MARCH AI

Retrospective views of a pleasant and historic Fen town

Trevor Bevis

ISBN 0 901680 50 8   COPYRIGHT © Trevor Bevis 1993

**Published by Trevor Bevis, 28 St. Peter's Road, March, Cambs.
PE15 9NA   Tel: (0354) 57286**

Printed by David J. Richards, 1 West Park Street, Chatteris, Cambs.
PE16 6AH   Tel: (0354) 692947

Whitemoor Marshalling Yards in post-war years
(Copyright Cambridge University Collection of Air Photographs)

A SAGA OF EVENTS

WHEN I came to March from Lincolnshire fifty years ago, it struck me as being a place of smells. Steam, grease and smoke from clanking locomotives mixed curiously with a repulsive stench rising from the river were the strange hallmarks of this town, though I will admit I rather liked the railway engines' nostalgic contribution. "Smoky March" made an incalculable contribution to the country's war effort what with countless trainloads of munitions, tanks, coal and foodstuffs automatically sorted at Whitemoor marshalling yard twenty-four hours a day for the War's duration. What old England would have done without March and its battalions of railmen, I really don't know.

¶ The steam and grease and sound of wagons being shunted on the hump have gone but what memories lurk in a generation's mind. The other smell has gone as well and the meandering river within the bounds of March, at any rate one of the prettiest in East Anglia, has turned a new leaf and affords a safe haven for cabin cruisers and longboats from far and near.

¶ How many towns have a park beside a river and such attractive walks as we have in West End and Nene Parade? Along the river banks and tree-lined paths with little gardens falling to the water's edge, in the company of centuries old houses and cottages one walks at peace in an embattled world. The little town, once an ugly and obnoxious child at last becomes of age and waxes beautiful with each passing year.

¶ Through the centuries men and women worked the soil of March and replenished their larders with fish and fowl in abundance. From the third century onwards human feet paced the reed fringed island in the Fens and scribes penned events surrounding our very own Saint Wendreda. The exploits of Hereward were surely spoken of by Mercians over open hearths and their pride knew no bounds in Tudor times which gave us the angel roof of wondrous beauty. The lean years of the drainage undertakers wreaked economic misery on the townspeople and a sadness and shame of the tragic disaster of 1849 sullied the town's progress for fifty years.

¶ Yet here we are in 1993, our little town set fair and square in the vastness of productive fen. Great changes have taken place and are taking place in a continuing saga of events which sank March into a pit of squalor then raised it to the heights of national fame.

¶ Strange it is indeed what fate will do.

Trevor Bevis
July 1993.

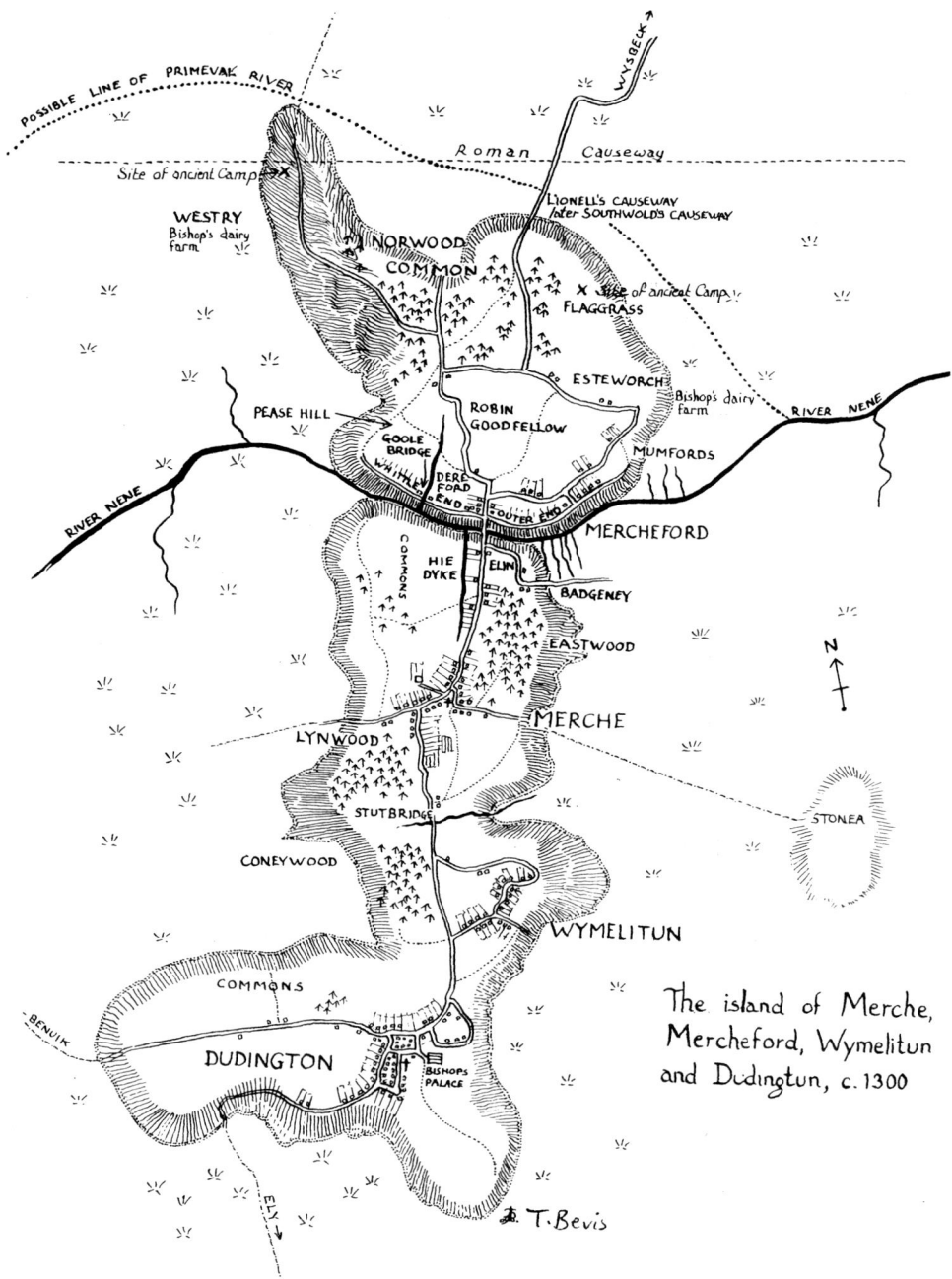

POSSIBLE LINE OF PRIMEVAL RIVER

Roman Causeway

WYSBECK

Site of ancient Camp X

WESTRY
Bishop's dairy farm

NORWOOD COMMON

LIONELL'S CAUSEWAY
later SOUTHWOLD'S CAUSEWAY

X Site of ancient Camp
FLAGGRASS

ESTEWORCH

Bishop's dairy farm

RIVER NENE

PEASE HILL

ROBIN GOODFELLOW

GOOLE BRIDGE

WHITLEY END

DERD FORD

OUTER END

MUMFORDS

MERCHEFORD

RIVER NENE

COMMONS

HIE DYKE

ELIN

BADGENEY

EASTWOOD

LYNWOOD

MERCHE

STUTBRIDGE

STONEA

CONEYWOOD

WYMELITUN

N

COMMONS

BENUIK

DUDINGTON

BISHOPS PALACE

ELY

T. Bevis

The island of Merche,
Mercheford, Wymelitun
and Dudingtun, c. 1300

The Romans marched here

MARCH stands on the edge of a Roman settlement which, had it been a few hundred yards nearer the boundary would place the town among the ranks of those dignified Latin bastions of Colchester, Lincoln and the rest. Slightly north-west of Grandford House on a slight rise is hidden the remains of a small Roman fortress and settlement served by the Fen Causeway, a military and commercial road sixty feet broad, by which Roman legions and traders had access to Fengate and the Carr Dike near Peterborough and the ancient Peddar's Way connecting to Norfolk's coast. The Fen Causeway near March skirts a second ancient site of Romano-British origin – at Flaggrass Hill – within the town's North-east boundary and about two miles north human skeletons have come to light. A skeleton from the Roman era was found on the new Berryfield estate and in various places in March over the course of almost three hundred years Roman coins were unearthed. A principal discovery of gold coins was the hoard discovered in Robingoodfellows Lane in the early 18th century. The Roman road passed through Whitemoor, the site of the famous railway marshalling yard recently replaced with a multi-million pound prison.

Contrary to belief that the town's name derives from the word "marsh" because of its fenny situation, March, stands on a dividing line between two ancient kingdoms – Mid Angles and Iceni – and was named "Merc" forming as it did part of the boundary. This is similar to the Welsh Marches (the boundary lands between England and Wales). The name is unique in the British Isles, but there is a Marche in Belgium (also depicting a boundary) and one in the United States of America (an Air Force base).

The ancient town of March situated in the heart of the Fens and formerly County Town of the old Isle of Ely constituency can be realistically traced to the mid-Saxon era (seventh century) and it is reasonably certain that a small community existed here at that time. Occupying an island almost thirty feet above sea level, the second largest island in the southern Fens after Ely, March shares its acres with the ancient villages of Doddington and Wimblington, themselves originally Saxon settlements. The former mentioned village was a country seat of the Bishop of Ely the estate covering 40,000 acres.

1

Not many communities can lay claim to possessing a church dedicated to a local saint. March has this distinct honour and it is largely due to Saint Wendreda (also known as Winifred) who came to the settlement in the late seventh century that the town justifiably claims such a long existence. Her decision to depart from Exning and live in the malarial Fens was two-fold: the area was known as The Holy Land of the English and it was fashionable for recluse, religious individuals to live in peace in areas richly endowed by nature. However, it was her desire to be at hand to assist in the spiritual and health requirements of the population. It is quite probable that Wendreda introduced Christianity to this part of the Fens; indeed, she may have been encouraged by Roman Orders to settle at Merc if only to discourage any Celtic influence spreading from Ancarig (Thorney) a few miles distant.

When she died Wendreda was buried at March but later her mortal remains were translated to Ely by order of King Ethelred the Second. There, within the abbey, her bones were enshrined with relics of other religious dignitaries including, it is thought, her sisters Saint Etheldreda and Saint Withburga of royal blood. The relic of Saint Wendreda is credited with a notable miracle. In 1016, Edmund Ironside, commander of the Saxon army, requested that the relic be conveyed at the head of the Saxon army on its way to do battle against a large gathering of Danes led by Cnut the Heathen. This was hopefully to enlist Divine help in defeating the invaders. As it turned out, the Saxons suffered a terrible, ignoble defeat at Ashington, Essex, hundreds of young noblemen falling before the furious onslaught of Danish sword and battleaxe.

Cnut, curious about the relic enclosed in a coffin adorned with precious and semi-precious stones, was told of the virtuous life of Wendreda. According to Saxon chronicles it was then that the miracle happened. Cnut was overcome with remorse for his heathen ways and immediately accepted the Christian faith, his example emulated by his followers. Out of respect for his new-found faith he ordered that Saint Wendreda's relic be enshrined in the major church at Canterbury, where it remained until about 1343. The relic was brought back to March and enshrined in the newly restored church dedicated to Wendreda's memory.

The church stands at the centre of the early Saxon settlement largely defined in the area known as Town End incorporating Knights End Road, Wimblington Road and The Avenue. This area is approximately a mile south of the River Nene (old course) which divided the town and played an important role in the parish economy. The outlying fens with their fisheries was important to the Saxon residents, harvesting as they did fish and wild fowl in abundance and mud and reed for building purposes. The island, six miles long and about two miles wide not only formed a sanctuary but was well afforested and served useful agricultural purposes. Narrow strips of land produced a variety of crops and there were extensive grazings for sheep, cattle and horses, and woods produced suitable food for swine. The land nearest the reed shore was usually well watered in winter and as a result became lush grazing for cattle set free from winter harbours on the island proper.

Many of the residents were employed at the fisheries on the river and in the fen and they contributed more than anyone else to the settlement's wellbeing. As the Church became predominantly obsessed with owning land and marsh, most of the local fishermen found themselves working under the authority of abbots and bishops who acquired marsh, pastures and meres with all the rights thereof. In about 1,000 A.D. Oswy and his wife Leofleda who possessed much of March and additional fen properties transferred the settlement and adjacent marsh to the Abbot of Ely when their son was accepted as a novice monk.

Broad Street, March c. 1900.

The magnificent 14th century steeple of St. Wendreda's church.

Dad's Army — 16th century style

A LIST made in about 1527 indicates that March and Doddington had in excess of two hundred subsidy men that could be called together for any type of emergency. A kind of mediaeval Home Guard, they were armed with halberts, swords, daggers and bows and they knew how to use them. Most had been trained in the use of weapons from a very early age and the inhabitants of March probably watched the men marching through the streets to the beat of a drum and went to their beds feeling more secure. It was much the same during the Second World War when the two battalions of March Home Guard – town and railway – periodically paraded through the streets, some armed only with bayonets!

For hundreds of years England placed much confidence in the local militia. From the days of the Hundred Years War, and in the times of French domination of Europe when Napoleon Bonaparte was a byword on everyone's lips, and when Herr Hitler sent his bombers into English skies, even above March, fit and able men of the townships and villages were ready to deal with foreign oppressors.

Nothing surpassed the spirit and resolution of Englishmen who, in days of yore, with their trusty bows and steel-tipped shafts earned more than passing respect in the battle fields of Europe. In 1572 an ancient law was reintroduced compelling every man under sixty years of age to possess a long bow of yew, ". . . and every man having a man child or men children in his house shall provide for all and teach them to shoot till they come to the age of seventeen. After that age they shall have a bow and four shafts."

Gunpowder was already in use but the English longbow continued to be a much respected, proved and reliable weapon and far more flexible than the Continental cross-bow. In accordance with the Act longbows were "three fingers thick and squared and seven feet long, well polished and without knots." All communities had at least a pair of butts and "no person above twenty-four years of age shall shoot with the light arrow at a distance under two hundred yards."

There were archery butts at March in 1552 and they cost 1s. 8d. to set up. A sheaf of arrows cost 5s. 6d. The town's ancient archery ground of about one rood was let to Laurence Wenden and Jeremy Chandler for a quarterly rent of four shillings. Guns are also

4

mentioned but were far from reliable, sometimes exploding in the handler's face! A steel-tipped shaft was capable of penetrating steel plate and transfixing a man's leg to his horse at a range of two hundred yards.

In 1557 John Shepherd of March bought a gun for seven shillings. It was kept in the town armoury. William Twayth purchased a sword and dagger for 6s. 8d: and in 1622 the town received delivery of two new muskets for 13s. 6d. The men of March must have looked very smart in 1600 sharing sparkling new breastplates. They also shared "a flaskyt and a tutch box" and probably looked enviously at William de Coward of Badgeney (died in 1609) who actually possessed his own "cote of plate." The town armoury bristled with armour, guns and swords, oh yes! and bows and shafts and pikes. One supposes the residents felt a sense of security with these items to hand and with water and marsh surrounding the island few strangers could safely approach this natural harbour, but Norwood residents kept wary eyes upon the Wisbech men who shared the commons with them.

As is always the case, war wreaks untold misery upon the taxpayer and March was heavily taxed in the Civil War. Three pounds in 1648 may not sound a large amount but when twopence would purchase bread and meat for a week and a five roomed house along West End built for little more than £12 just think what £3 would buy! An entry in the churchwardens' book states: "Received by William Neale of Mr. Girling the sum of £10, part of the £14 3s. 4d. allowed by the toune committee for monies spent in times of allarum." This amount may have been levied by Parliamentarian authority at the time when the Isle of Ely was fortified against the King. The Restoration of the Monarchy brought about a great change. Oliver Cromwell had died and his gentle son had had the good sense to return to farming at Wicken. No more cavalry patrols, no more military taxation. The fortress at March was left to decay but its name lives on in the new estate near the Neale Wade school.

A few men from our pleasant island in the Fens died serving the King. Charitable hands were extended to them and the war widows. One, an ex-Cavalier, living near March suffered terrible wounds from which he died. His friends organised a petition in support of his wife and family:

"Wee the inhabitants of Doddington doe certify to whome it may concern that Thomas Sperry late which he lived at Doddington aforesaid deceased, was formerly about two years eldest sergeant under Sir Marmaduke Rayden in his owne company . . . The said

Thomas Sperry at Ogdean in Hampshire in actual service received such pestiferous wounds that he could not be cured neither in hospital insomuch the malignity of the infectious wounds did so corode the flesh from all his neck and face upon which languishing condicon he wasted all his estate . . . in seeking a cure but could not obtayne it. The said Thomas had left his wife and fower very small children succoulesse. Also that Thomas (in Cromwell's time) was long kept in prison for bearing armes." Some witnesses of Sergeant Sperry's sad condition, army men as well as "feelow sueffers," added their names to the petition. Let us hope that his wife and the succourless mites benefitted from the appeal. The aftermath of the Civil War was a national problem felt by thousands for many years. In October 1662, Parliament awarded retired Cavaliers and their widows pensions of £5 per annum, but if one had fought for our intrepid Fenman, Oliver Cromwell, then one could hope for no benefit at all. Of all wars civil strife is the bitterest, most brutal and merciless as is well illustrated in the recent troubles of states within the former country of Yugoslavia.

A carrier's van pictured along Station Road c. 1900.

March Guilds

I N THE Middle Ages guilds existed to benefit members fallen on hard times. It frequently happened. Guilds were usually attached to the Church and, indeed, were benefactors, some being builders in their own right, erecting splendid chapels and richly adorning them. The number of mediaeval guilds serving a community indicated opulence and high status of a town. Some, known as frith guilds, were of a secular nature and were the forerunners of present day friendly societies.

March had seven guilds in olden times and from that number we might deduce that the town played an eminent role in the Fens. The guilds were connected with Saint Wendreda's church and dedicated to Holy Trinity, Saint Anne, Saint John the Baptist, Saint Christopher, Saint Mary, Saint Peter and Saint Wendreda. The guild of Saint John may have been instrumental in the erection of the church tower, the groined passageway beneath showing an appropriate emblem, an eagle, carved on a boss.

Apparently the guild of Saint Wendreda was the town's oldest organisation, likely founded in the 14th century to honour the enshrinement of the relic within the church. It is the only guild in Britain known to have left a Will, whereby "if it shall fall into decay by reason of pestilence or any other source of failure, the goods thereof shall be given towards the fabric of the chapel of March."

Guild certificates referring to this ancient institution clearly state that the relic of the saint lay enshrined in the chapel and that the guild had been established "in honour of Saint Wyndreda which was removed to the chapel there." Some guilds accummulated considerable wealth which helped the community in various ways, as was evidenced in the activities of the Guild of Holy Trinity at Wisbech, so embued with valuable possessions it even maintained the flood defences and was later incorporated into the Corporation.

The March Guild of Saint Christopher, founded during the 15th century, was one of the more important guilds of the town. One of its early members, Mr. Kersey, bequeathed his wealth equally "to every guild within the town of March." His death signalled extensive activities to commemorate his influence in the town. At his "obit" all brethren and sisters were summoned to Saint Wendreda's to donate money in memory of the deceased. The curate was paid to recite prayers for the repose of Mr. Kersey's soul for a period of not less than a month. It was an important condition that a deceased member be honoured by the brethren and sisters over a period of time and a rota was arranged for members known as lightbearers to attend to the candles on the various altars lit with the deceased in mind. If the curate was absent they would recite the usual prayers.

The Guild of St. Christopher kept a book to record memoranda. In it a few of the earlier members are mentioned: John Southwold, farmer (probably commemorated in Southwold's Causeway, Elm Road), and Mary, his wife; John Spencer, shipbuilder with premises on the River Nene, and his wife, Alice, etc. The entries were written in contracted Latin in 1472.

A typical entry: "Memorandum – the light keepers of St. Christopher, John Walsham, John Neal, Thomas Southwold of Whittlesey End (West End), Thomas Southwold of the bridge (the earliest mention of a bridge at Mercheford), Richard Coward – in the year of Our Lord 1495. There remains in John Neal's hands and (in the hands of) Thomas Southwold for the keeping of Saint Christopher's light 3s. 4d. and 21 lbs. of wax . . ." Wax for producing candles was expensive. It sometimes fell to the priest and curate to make candles for use on major and minor altars but guilds provided their own.

Every guild held an annual High Day. Members of St. Christopher's guild celebrated theirs on the Monday after the Feast of the Epiphany. In 1530 there were thirty members, not a great number but they were well heeled. It was a closed shop really, the members meeting in the guidhall and all the town's guilds had their altars in the parish church, usually before the pillars in the aisles. These were colourfully draped and candles burned constantly upon them.

Desecration and destruction fell upon the town after 1546. Monasteries, churches and guilds became prime targets in the King's desire to "Reform" and restrict the old order of things. Guildhalls were dispossessed and rituals expunged from parish life. The new order introduced poverty and confusion which lasted almost two hundred years. The guildhall of St. Christopher was given to the town and renamed "toune house", similar to another building adjacent to the church which was renamed "treasure house." The last few days in the existence of March guilds witnessed doleful procedures for the winding up of the organisations. Not all items were handed over to the commissioners. "Fyve sylver sponys and two masers" (wooden cups) turned up in safer times and were kept for church use.

Populations waxed and waned

I N THE fourteenth century the country was ravaged by pestilence known as the Black Death. It decimated populations as never before, people literally falling to the ground where they stood. Two thousand clergy in Norfolk and Suffolk perished and forty seven of the hundred monks at Saint Albans gave up the ghost in the wake of this relentless destroyer of mankind. At Ely a whole street was wiped out and other parts of the diocese, too, felt the cold grip of the scourge, although the Fens being a watery region with fewer visitors probably fared better than other regions. Many years later, when it was all over, the country seriously depopulated, villages abandoned and acute shortages of skilled labour that church building had to be delayed for years, monuments began to spring up in the form of thanksgiving for deliverance. Flat topped towers, like that of Saint Wendreda's, were capped with spires beheld by inhabitants as a finger of supplication pointing to heaven.

Plague and pestilence in some form or other have always stalked the world. Certainly the town of March did not escape these things, although there was a tendency for the occasional dread visitations to be regarded as quite normal and one took a chance. At March between 1560 and 1570 there were 334 live births and 200 deaths. When the town showed signs of expanding in 1600 the population stood at around a thousand. Between 1600 and 1625, 383 baptisms were recorded in the town as against 634 burials at Town End. That was a bad period and the town's population, instead of increasing, actually declined. From 1625 to 1650, 960 infants were lovingly carried to the Norman font at Saint Wendreda's church. The town bier was well used, too, no fewer than 793 bodies carried over the same period.

In August 1638 there was an average number of deaths (ten), but when harvesting commenced the mortality rate suddenly and alarmingly increased. Eight deaths occurred in September and that was followed by eleven in October. Twelve burials took place during November and December but in January and February, due no doubt to the rigours of winter, twenty–six graves had to be prepared. In the course of a year March suffered 90 deaths from a population of little more than a thousand. Whole families were decimated. The Adams' first lost mother Jone, then daughters Mary and Katherine. Finally father was placed beside them. Two Neale girls succumbed to the "pest" and a little later their father was borne to his grave. John Shephard lost five members of his family that year and Hugh Vickers listened to the mournful knell of the church bell for his son and two daughters.

Three centuries ago hygiene was unheard of. There were no vitamins nor pre-packed foods. Herbs were plentiful but medical science was limited and crude. Variety of food was not as plentiful as now, but cabbages, peas and garlic could be found in most seventeenth century kitchens. Recipe books existed too. Mrs. Oliver Cromwell published one but I think it would be hardly acceptable nowadays. The poor managed to exist on dismal diets and that probably contributed to tragic results during the onslaught of disease. They simply could not summon the strength to resist. The number of baptised infants interred in Saint Wendreda's churchyard must amount to hundreds. It is probable that a good many, and some adults too, were buried in their back gardens. It was a tendency in times of severe plague to do that after a service in the house, to try to minimise the risk of spreading disease. At least forty home burials occurred at Peterborough and there is no reason to doubt that that practice happened at March during the worst of visitations.

In comparatively modern times infant mortality at March occurred with sickening frequency. In 1814 twenty-six infants were recorded in the register of deaths. By a remarkable coincidence exactly the same number of infant deaths occurred the following year, and that does not take into account the unrecorded number of stillborn babes who were usually buried at other places other than churchyards. Even in the mid twentieth century the premature stillborn were placed in cardboard boxes, such as a shoebox, and buried on waste land in the middle of March for instance. Many earlier burials of baptised infants were paid for out of the parish funds.

How fortunate we are in this so-called enlightened age that infant deaths are very rare, thanks to modern, hygienic conditions and scientific and medical advances which contribute to a longer and happier life span. Such advances however can have their penalties, such as over populated areas aggravated by man-made environmental pollution which our ancestors never experienced. The modern phenomenon called recession with attendant financial pressures is a direct result of the desire to produce materials for increasing world-wide populations with slowing mortality rate in the western sphere at least. And more significantly still the poor are with us.

Extracts from March Registers

AMONG the prized possessions of an ancient church are its registers, usually spanning many centuries. At one time these valuable documents were kept in church safes, but now they are more likely to be kept in county records offices and at recognised local museums. It is not unusual to discover that some pages have been misused and even cut out by over-enthusiastic researchers of family histories and the towns and villages where the documents had been preserved for so long are the poorer.

St. Wendreda's church, March, possessed no less than thirty registers of which *The Booke of Marche* is the earliest. It contains baptisms, burials and marriages, the first entry having been entered on March 25th 1558 by the curate, Nicolas Stutewile, who continued in that capacity until 1599.

The entries of this particular register are impressively immaculate but others dating to the 17th and 18th centuries were less labouriously executed. Centuries ago illiteracy was a common and expected thing, a fact emphasised in the matrimonial entries of three hundred and more years ago when the contracting parties were able only to apply their binding marks in the form of an "X" - somewhat shaky examples too, due perhaps to the customary nerves!

Another interesting feature in the marriage registers of our old church can be observed in the nature of the oft-times unusual employment of the bridegroom. Most seem to have been labourers, but also noted are bricklayers, farmers, carpenters, an Officer of Excise, a common brewer, a boatwright, cordwainers and watermen, the latter, one assumes, plying their trade on the network of Fenland's waterways, transporting an assortment of materials which included gravel, timber. corn and coal to Peterborough, Chatteris, Outwell and Wisbech. Well-known March families were entered in the registers and two Guyhirn families, a Culy girl on the writer's side and a Tegerdine man who eloped and were hastily married at St. Wendreda's church in the early 1700's before the irate parents could catch them up!

Of equal interest, the Churchwardens' books contain numerous entries, these officers then being the chief administrators of the town, distributing monies for bridge and causeway repairs as well as a twopence or a sixpence to vagrants, an unfortunate race of men, women and children cast upon the roadside, ex-soldiers, sailors, the halt and blind. They called upon the churchwardens and constables and received a little money from the church coffers. Then they were ordered to depart from the town.

The earliest entry in the Churchwardens' book is dated 1542: "Payd to ye goldsmith in part payment for a pyx and a crystratory of sylver, ivj li." It is in these accounts that one learns of "Sam's wife," who seems to have been a woman of integrity married to mine host of the Sweet Briar. March will always be in debt to her. An account was entered in 1547 "to Sam's wife for drynkynge, the first time the emags (images) were plucked down." She received a shilling. At that important time of English history, the country at the crossroads and the Dissolution of the monasteries well under way, the original high altar at St. Wendreda's was broken up as was probably the religious shaft and its figure on the town's Stone Cross. Images which adorned the several inferior altars in the church, too, were taken down and destroyed in accordance with national fervour which swept the country "to reform the Church, not to destroy" as Henry the Eighth had declared.

Sam's wife, God bless her soul, had provided a sumptuous dinner "when we drew ye obit out of ye booke for going to Ely when we carried the plait." The King's Commissioners having produced an inventory of the church treasures were suitably impressed with the lady's talent for cooking. The town fathers took advantage of the occasion to tell them that the beautiful roof could do no harm to the new style of faith and, in any case, if the heavy oak figures were removed the upper part of the church might well collapse around the congregation. The structural principles were so sophisticated. The Commissioners turned a blind eye to the carved angels and martyrs, but it was required of the churchwardens to remove the images set before the pillars and elsewhere, dismantle the shrine containing the relic of St. Wendreda and destroy all monuments and books relevant to pre-Dissolution practices.

It was in 1547, the old church looking rather bare, that a new high altar was installed but it shared the same fate as the first, being removed in 1558 during the Reformation and replaced with a new communion table. The roodloft had already been deprived of its religious figures and managed to survive until 1566 when the town's odd-job man, usually employed on the waterside, was engaged to take it down. The loft had probably been incorporated into the beautifully carved and painted screen which, with the famous memorial roof, formed a distinctive and inspiring feature to many pilgrims that visited March in the summer months.

Up and down the country angels were taken down from resplendent ceilings, leaving that at March intact. Norfolk and Suffolk has several fine examples of single and double hammerbeam roofs, some mutilated, and one or two similar to March, but it is the experts' opinion that the roof at March is the finest example of late mediaeval craftsmanship in the whole of Europe.

One day, not many years ago, the writer unexpectedly came across a fine old book, once the property of St. Wendreda's church, and which was the means of introducing him to numerous events which transpired in the town centuries ago. The dilapidated volume contains no less than 750 parchment pages meticulously hand written and span the years from 1540 to 1680. Certain entries referred to long vanished March properties and wills by which the town's poor had benefitted. There are also accounts of town and church collections, some monies despatched to relieve distressed people living in London and other places visited by the plague. A great deal of information related to the church bells and repairs to the building which had taken place over a period of one-hundred-and-forty years.

Himself a campanologist (bellringer to you!) the writer had not infrequently experienced frustration at his being unable to fill in gaps concerning bells at the church. Cole, in his manuscript, refers to a ring of five bells at March in the 18th century. Who had cast them? The ancient book provided the answer. Near an item referring to payment to ringers for ringing the bells on London Plot Day (Guyfawkes) were items concerning the bells written in 1670. Someone had received payment for preparations prior to the removal of old and worn bells. The churchwarden himself had his cart loaded with one or more bells and then transported them to the bell foundry at Haddenham.

The bellfounder, Christopher Graye, took up his breaker's hammer and reduced the bells to fragments. (Two had been cast at Thetford earlier that century). The pieces were introduced to the furnace and, with the addition of new metal, five brand new bells were "run" for March church. This operation cost the parish £42. A modern ring of bells complete with frame would cost in the region of £40,000! In the meantime, a Mr. George, carpenter, had made and installed an oak frame in the church tower and the new bells were loaded onto the churchwarden's cart and conveyed to March. Mr. George was paid £17 for his services, as much as would build a four roomed cottage along West End. Then came the task of raising the bells to belfry height and seating them in their respective bays. This was heavy work and required the services of Thomas Dawson, a kind of gangmaster, who went around the town rounding up able bodied men and boys and assembling them at the church where they worked several days hauling the bells into the tower. The bells gave good service until 1801 when they were taken down and hauled along Bell Metal Lane which was joined to Badgeney Road to be loaded onto a barge, then towed along the River Nene by Dobbin to Downham Market. There they were broken up and recast into the existing musical ring of six by Thomas Osborn, bellfounder. The new bells were hung at St. Wendreda's church the following year. The metal of bells up to four hundred years old reverberate in the metallic melodies travelling lightly above the town. Long may they continue to laud the nuptial rite and remind souls of the spiritual destiny of mankind. It is amazing what one can learn from the magic of a long lost book!

Making up for missed opportunities

THE HISTORY of March is epitomised in its oldest and grandest building, St. Wendreda's church, a mixture of conflicting and harmonising styles. Viewed from the steeple the town is seen as a green oasis in a flat landscape almost void of trees. Walking through its streets reveals a hotchpotch of architectural designs, styles of plainness and styles of artificial and natural beauty.

Elevated on its former island of boulder clay some twenty-eight feet above the prolific fenland and neatly cleaved in two by the River Nene (old course), anciently called Le Ee, March is really two communities brought together by the former importance of its main highway – the river.

About one thousand years ago, people began to place more importance to the riverside than the original settlement area, Merc, in the vicinity of St. Wendreda's church. They named the new settlement Mercheford after the ford crossing the river which was much higher than now. This settlement quickly outstripped Merc which has always retained its "village" environment. In 1287 there were 77 tenants and owners living along the waterside. The area between the ford to a distance about half-a-mile south of the town bridge was high marsh, and because it tended to be wet hardly any buildings stood there. The Causeway was continually being repaired and the churchwardens were constantly being asked in the 16th century to finance the road's maintenance costs. The two communities shared the same church, oldest part dating to 1250, as well as the market place, probably on the site of the mediaeval Stone Cross which was fairly free of drainage problems. The present market place was officially formed as a viable trading area in 1671, mainly because of the close proximity of the river, warehouses and wharfs and shops.

Deeply confined between steep grassed banks the river is thought to have been excavated through the island by Romans anxious to protect the Fen Causeway, a little further north, from the inconvenience of floods in winter. The old Roman road from Denver, Norfolk to Fengate, Peterborough, served a useful military and commercial purposes and lay close to a primeval river which was discovered between Ring's End and March. The Fen Causeway crossed Whitemoor and served the Roman settlement at Grandford.

The town has a fascinating history spanning at least fourteen centuries. A number of important events are etched into its past: The coming of Wendreda (saint) in the late seventh century; her translation to Ely; six centuries later the relic's translation from Canterbury to March; the restoration and embellishment of the parish church and erection of the famous memorial angel roof; the coming of the railway in 1846; the disastrous effect of disease upon the population in 1849/50; and the emergence of the town as the administrative centre of the old Isle of Ely.

Eighteen-forty-nine was the worst year that March has ever known, leaving a stain on its progress well visible into the twentieth century. No fewer than 441 inhabitants died within a twelve month period as a result of neglected drainage and contaminated water supplies. According to government inspectors March had the worst mortality rate per head of population in the whole of the country.

The translation of St. Wendreda's relic from Canterbury to March in circa 1341 was of enormous benefit to the town. For more than two centuries the shrine played a major role in the town's economy, many pilgrims visiting March on their way to Peterborough, Ely and the major shrine at Walsingham in Norfolk. Much of March's mediaeval economy was based on the town's numerous fisheries, several owned by successive bishops of Ely and abbots of East Dereham and Ramsey. Each year all able-bodied men from the town's five wards took turns erecting dams in the river and dragged nets along its considerable parish length. Residents were obliged to forego meat on Wednesdays and Fridays and ate fish instead. In the 16th century one man received special dispensation from the Archbishop of Canterbury to eat meat on those days as fish made him ill.

The town's economy was further enhanced through extensive common land managed by Fenreves, a tough, unyielding type of person. Here inhabitants with commonable cottages were allowed to graze large herds of cattle, flocks of sheep and much valued Fen horses which were prized by the nation's army. There were also large acreages of beechwood ideal for hogs. Norwoodside common was shared with Wisbech, an arrangement which generated many disputes between the two towns. March possessed much more marsh than did Wisbech which suffered from sea and fresh water floods. The boundaries of March extended as far as Coates in the west and Elm to the north. The men of March earned themselves a notorious reputation for luring neighbouring cattle across the boundaries, then setting them free on payment of a fine! The matter came to a head in 1586 when the butchers of March, resentful of Wisbech's frequent intrusion upon Norwoodside, sallied forth onto the common and set about Wisbech sheep, maiming them and even slitting the throats of some.

This resulted in a serious dispute between the towns, and the Bishop who had had more than enough of the "lawless men of March" was obliged to intercede. He placated angry Wisbechians by sending a strong warning to March in which he said he would personally visit the town and deliver such a sermon the erring parishioners would wish him never to repeat the like again! This set off a pattern of innumerable elements of friction between the towns, seen in later years as lighthearted rivalry. Happily both places have mellowed.

WORKHOUSE AN ORNAMENT TO THE TOWN

THE eighteenth century was a disastrous period for the Isle of Ely. Gradual drainage of wet fen deprived wildfowlers and fishermen of their livelihood. Newly drained fen could not be worked for a length of time and, as a result, a large number of vagrant poor was deposited with the parish. In 1785-6 Cambridgeshire had one in ten adults in workhouses (331); the Isle of Ely had one in three (665), an average of 60 per workhouse in the county. (March could accommodate a hundred and Wisbech one-hundred-and-fifty). In winter the idle and vagrant poor drifted into the workhouses. It was difficult to get rid of them when better weather prevailed.

At March the mediaeval guildhall was used as a workhouse from 1575 until 1823, the year it was pulled down and purpose-built premises provided "replete with every convenience; an ornament to the town . . ." In connection with this a rent bill of £440 annually alarmed the inhabitants and drastic action was brought to bear. This was in the form of a very efficient though one fears impassionate Keeper, who quickly sized up the situation and undertook to make the inmates' tasks really arduous, and to farm them at a lesser sum per head than was possible elsewhere. The Keeper was given seventeen acres of land next to the workhouse, rate and tax free. This man whom some in our own day and age would think was born a century or so before his time vigorously carried out the agreement, making the inmates work for their keep, so much so, that the able-bodied were glad to leave at the earliest opportunity. The result? The rent bill decreased to £100 in the first year.

From the inauguration of its notable Holy Trinity Guild in the 14th century, Wisbech was always known as a trier with considerable success in fields of industry, agriculture and horticulture and its port was well known throughout the Baltic. For the last two hundred years March lacked vision and adopted apathetic attitudes, its councils being content to wait and see. The town anaesthetised itself and the fact that it has got on as well as it has and superseded Wisbech on a few points is no credit to its successive councils. The plural slips off the pen quite effortlessly when recalling the town's missed opportunities.

Essentially a market town with long and traditional agricultural ties, centrally positioned in an area rightly known as the nation's larder, it was purely luck that its greatest industry, the railway (now sadly defunct) saved it from further deterioration. The worst period for March was between 1830-1850 and it seems these regretful decades set the town marking time for many years.

In the mid nineteenth century March comprised an archipelago of islands intersected by numerous ditches filled to the brim with debris and filth of the worst kind. A directory hailed March as a progressive town; wealthy residents lived in elegant Georgian houses mainly in the High Street with metalled surface, but it failed to mention the miserable paupers existing in hovels standing for most part in stagnant pools of water and along tracks with ruts eighteen inches deep. They smoked opium and indulged in unseemly habits to relieve them from depression. They slept in airless, windowless rooms, some only four to five feet high. A government inspector was horrified to find thirteen sleeping in a single room and observed women struggling with pails of contaminated water from pumps hundreds of yards from their homes.

Foul waste surrounded them and poisoned water seeped from cess pits into private wells. Animal refuse from slaughter houses was literally burnt in backyards, adding to the stench which pervaded the town. Drainage did not take place in the normal manner. The town drained through the process of evaporation. As many as twelve cottages shared a single privy and almost half of the population had no toilet facilities at all. Typhoid, ague, cholera, atrophy and diarrhoea thrived in these conditions and ended the lives of 441 residents over a twelve-month period ending Michaelmas 1849. St. Wendreda's churchyard filled so rapidly that the Bell Field opposite was utilised as an emergency burial ground, the first interments taking place before it was consecrated.

This terrible tragedy was largely due to the local authority's unwillingness to provide clean, fresh water and install a suitable sewage system. The authority relied on an antiquated system in the form of the ancient Hythe, a mediaeval waterway into which refuse and waste was thrown and eventually seeped into the River Nene. The Hythe and the river were at the heart of the problem, the latter receiving waste, etc., from householders living in Whittle End and Nene Parade. It took a few hundred deaths and better men to force the local authority to enclose the Hythe and obtain fresh water from near the railway and pipe it into every house in the town. But it was not until several years later that the Council gave its consent for provision of an efficient drainage and sewage system.

From the early years of the nineteenth century until well into the twentieth century the affairs of March were decreed by successive councils, a large proportion of members with more than a passing interest in agricultural and related matters. This was the tendency in the Isle of Ely where farmers were reluctant to see too much progress, especially industriallywise, for fear of losing workers to higher paid jobs. At March this representation had a suppressive effect on any industrial hopes related to a fluctuating population of between 6,500 and 12,000 (postwar) over a period of 130 years.

THE FAMOUS RAILWAY MARSHALLING YARDS

Capitalists were attracted to the Fens by the assurance of incomparable yields of crops from the newly drained fields. At March and Chatteris farmers hired women and children to deliberately trample upon the young shoots to delay growth. In the second half of the 19th century some fields were so fertile that three crops could be grown in the season without as much as a furrow. The farmers' employees received insignificant wages for their efforts. Fear of a mass exodus from the land to more lucrative jobs encouraged land owners to occupy positions of prominence on various agricultural boards and even more important, as representatives on the Urban

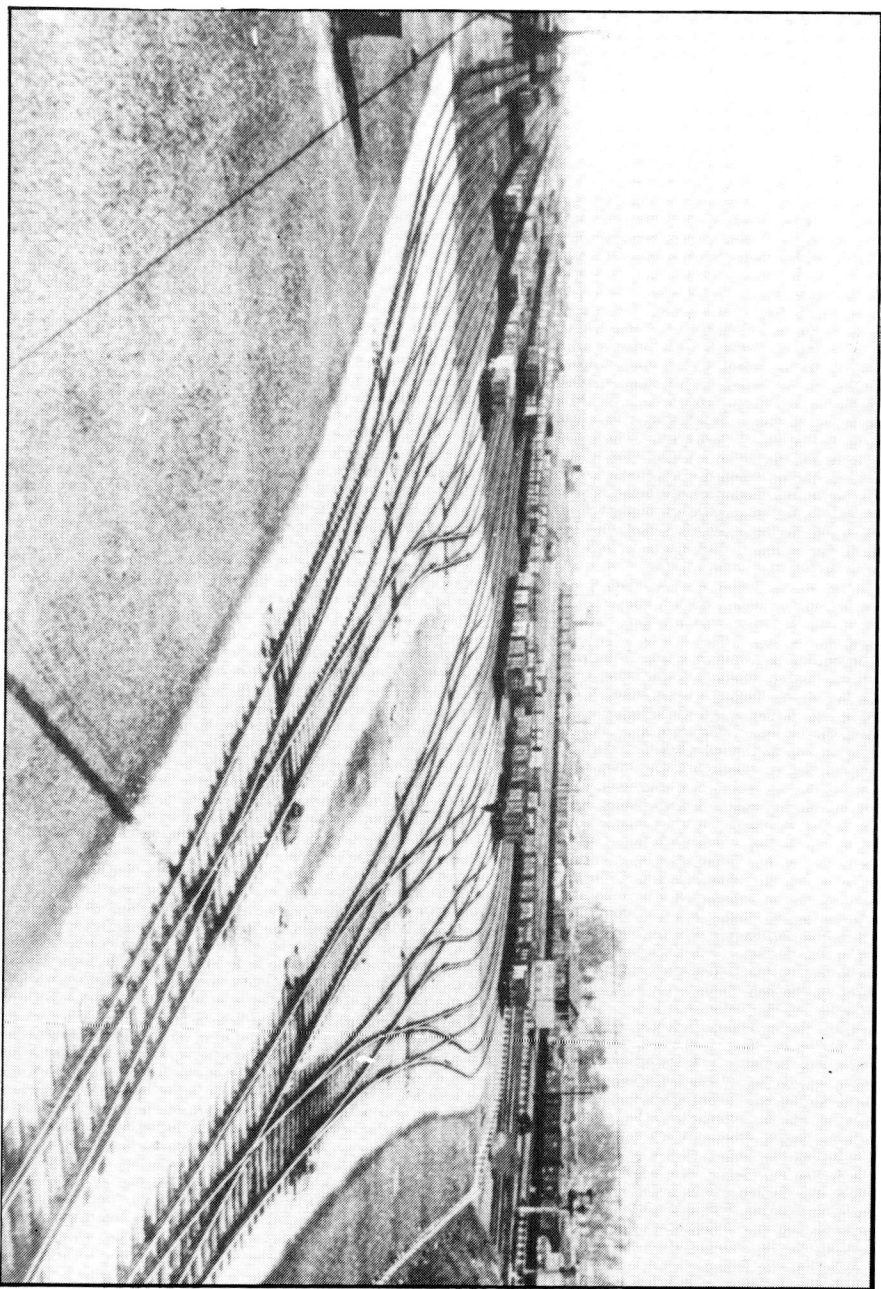

New "Down" marshalling yard, Whitemoor. April 15th, 1934.
(Colin Bedford's collection of railway photographs)

The railway station at March, first quarter of the 20th century.

District Council. Little was done to encourage alternative employment. That regressive attitude is best examined inasmuch that the council was reluctant to accept the railway centre's development on the town's doorstep. As it turned out they had no choice and the marshalling yards at Whitemoor, the largest in Europe, and at one time during the 1939-45 World War, the greatest complex of its kind in the world, made its home at March. This enterprise was a stroke of good fortune for March although it did not really deserve it. The Eastern Counties railway company had hoped to develop the railway centre at Wisbech and link it to the port. The ardent Wisbech banker and Quaker, Lord Peckover had agreed to sell land at North Brink to the railway company but he imposed an unacceptable condition: the railway centre, he stipulated, must not work on Sundays.

At March, lack of industry had caused the population to decline by an alarming twelve per cent. The Council, concerned at what might happen if they rejected the railway company's request to develop the centre at March, agreed that the company could do so. The council grudgingly agreed to provide homes for railway employees, but the first residences were situated a good two miles from Whitemoor and the railway staff had to cycle through the centre of the town to get to work. Whitemoor railway complex was one of the chief reasons that March developed in a northerly direction. The other reason was the establishment of the County Hall (Fenland Hall) in County Road. That was why several professional individuals in the county preferred to travel by rail to March in order that they might conveniently pursue business at the Isle of Ely administrative headquarters.

The railway came to March in the mid 1840's and the first yards developed between Creek Road crossing and that at Station Road. A depot lay just off the present station. During the late 1920's and early 1930's Whitemoor really came into its own, the "Up" yard and "Down" yard equipped with the latest German technology. If all the lines were filled end to end more than 17,000 wagons could be accommodated. The new depot accommodated a large number of steam locomotives and in later years various classifications of diesel locomotives.

The marshalling yard reached its peak between 1935 and 1950 when, especially during the Second World War, every twenty-four hours between 350 and 400 trains, mainly munitions, war equipment, and fuel, etc., were marshalled and distributed to all parts of the United Kingdom. Hitler's experts were very interested in the day to day workings of Whitemoor, the Germans having partly equipped it.

Occasionally German reconnaisance aircraft flew above the complex at night. Disruptive bombing and strafing of the yards' approaches occurred now and then but thankfully no real effort was made to eliminate it by blanket bombing, it being said that the enemy hoped one day to use it themselves! There were no fewer than thirty-nine bombing incidents centred upon March and district, and twenty enemy and allied aircraft crashed in the vicinity. Early in the war bombs from a German aircraft struck property along Norwood Road and killed a number of people, injuring others. A flying bomb, probably targeted on London, eighty miles distant, lost its way and harmlessly exploded on the March boundary. Among the strange occurences which happened within the little Fen town was that when German airmen were seen actually sitting patiently on the town bridge waiting to be picked up and interrogated!

March has reason to be grateful to a young Australian pilot who, having seen the crew bale out of the stricken Stirling bomber, stayed at the controls and somehow managed to guide the aircraft above the housetops before it crashed onto a field just west of St. Wendreda's church. The airman, Pilot Officer Jim Hocking, was instantly killed and kerosene from the 'plane spilled onto a Royal Observer Corps post seriously burning a member of staff.

March had a golden opportunity to urge industry to take advantage of the railway centre with connections with all parts of the country. Sites adjoining Whitemoor were ideally placed, but no-one seemed interested and the chance of a lifetime was lost. Had industry moved in, at least part of the railway might well have survived. When the unthinkable happened and the marshalling yards were closed leaving a slender link still open to the rail network, a few factories and small units were constructed close to the railway site. The largest development to take place was the building of a huge multi-million pound prison at Whitemoor which, at the time of severe recession, one supposes was welcome, the staff adding handsomely to the town's population, which stands at the time of writing in the region of 17,000.

On the face of things March has not done too badly. Despite all its historical shortcomings it is a pleasant little town with several amenities, a reasonable shopping centre, an indoor swimming pool and a host of clubs and societies. The tree-lined river is probably its greatest asset coursing past the Park which is right in the centre of the town. March even has a marina which affords direct access to hundreds of miles of navigable Fen waterways popular with anglers from considerable distances. Several housing estates materialised during the past twenty years, proof that many people prefer to reside in a small town rather than the city. Here, the environment is generally unpolluted and the generous canopy of sky with its changing patterns of mountain ranges and pony tails, the open fields and those matchless sunsets and sunrises saturate everything with strong senses of freedom, expression and independence, the ancient birthrights of a true Fenman.

Summer cruising on the River Nene.

Ancient Stones

Perhaps the mystery surrounding the ancient Stone Cross at March is penetrable after all. The mediaeval base which has stood for five hundred years in The Avenue inspired much speculation in the past hundred years or so. The stepped structure formed the base of a slender stone shaft supporting possibly a figure of Christ or another religious figure similar to the ancient calvary near the lychgate at Doddington. There the cross was discovered by a former Rector, Reverend Ridge, who recovered it from a field where it had been hidden by a priest at the time of the Dissolution.

Some have said that March Stone Cross existed before St. Wendreda's church was built and that it was the place where people worshipped before they were given a roof for their heads. That is not true as the earliest part of the church dates from about 1250 and the cross which is Perpendicular was erected about two-hundred-and-fifty-years later. At one time there were in the region of 10,000 stone and wooden crosses scattered up and down the country but they are uncommon nowadays. Churchyard crosses had their beginning in the fifth century. From a simple interlaced Celtic design they developed in design and size up to the first half of the 16th century. Seven-hundred years ago they were not only visible in churchyards but were introduced to the roadsides as well. It was common practice to build them by the wayside from the 14th century onwards, some crosses decorated with florated heads in the shape of a cross, or supporting a religious figure as does that at Stretham, near Ely. Others possessed little religious significance and had shafts terminating into a point or surmounted with a stone sphere, like that at Lavenham, Suffolk.

Stepped structures are really open-air pulpits and were known as "preaching crosses" to remind people of their divine relationship. They were usually erected by various Orders of Friars who were sent out from their establishments as spiritual ambassadors for their respective Orders. Sometimes these colourful and quick witted characters combined these excursions with business, the friaries enjoying certain material privileges beyond the jurisdiction of Monarch and Parliament, and learned to thrive exceedingly well upon the natural resources of the countryside. In that way the preachers, attired in course materials of black, brown and white habits, formed very useful links between their superiors and the laity. They were regarded in an enviable and vindictive light by church clergy who regarded the friars as trespassers and would never allow them to speak within the confines of churches and churchyards. The friars were a profound nuisance to parish priests whose authority they tended to deliberately undermine. Undeterred and with full support of the great preaching Orders the friars gave their sermons and often attracted crowds from miles around. In a good many places they even provided counter attraction at country fairs and were justly famous for verbal fireworks and forthrightness – usually at the local priest's expense!

Not to be outdone by parochial priests' attitudes, the Orders decreed that crosses be erected upon steps to enable the nomad preachers to address people from advantageous positions. The spiritual lords were careful to ascertain that the crosses be sited on or as near as possible to the place where markets were held. Rarely did they erect crosses away from centres where people habitually met and where assemblies generally took the form of a commercial nature.

The Friars could only erect preaching crosses at towns and villages over which they exercised some authority. The nearest religious establishments to March were those at Chatteris, Ramsey, Thorney and Outwell, but it is doubtful that those places had anything to do with the Stone Cross at March.

At the beginning of the fifteenth century March extended a limb in a northerly direction towards Mercheford and it was a matter of time before the two communities which shared the same church would join themselves as one. This expansion followed the ridge along the existing Avenue where the track slightly descended to the area known as high marsh as far as the town bridge. A market of some sort existed somewhere and it is the writer's opinion that the Stone Cross may well mark the site of the mediaeval market only just upon the higher ground and about half way between Merch and Mercheford.

It is reasonable to suppose the vanished shaft supported a cross or a carving. If this was the case then the Stone Cross was erected for the convenience of the preaching friars. This is substantiated in that the shaft, as in the case of thousands of similar obelisks of a religious nature, was removed and probably destroyed. All this would be done in accordance with orders from the Bishop of Ely that all memorials, altars and images and records of shrines, etc., etc. be removed from sight in the name of the Reformation.

At the time of the Dissolution and Reformation incalculable works of great beauty were removed from parish churches and the majority of major ecclesiastical buildings allowed to decay. Can there be any alternative reason as to why the March Cross is missing? Like that at Doddington it may have been carefully dismantled and buried in a field not far away. One feels justified in the belief that the Stone Cross was the focal point where people gathered to purchase market wares while a friar sermonised from the steps.

At the close of the fifteenth century thousands of preaching-cum-market crosses existed in the country. The cross at March was one of the last erected, few, if any of the stepped type being built after 1510. The Reformation, gathering momentum, wrote finis on the ancient, weathered stones of wayside pulpits, and these were replaced by "crosses" of a more practical and wordly nature, usually named after such commodities as butter and wool, and protected by roofs supported by pillars like that at Whittlesey, beneath which traders offered produce.

The river at March, once an important commercial artery, influenced the town fathers in their selection of the market site in 1671, notwithstanding the gaul of Wisbech — the self-styled capital — which unsuccessfully opposed the venture. The Stone Cross had had its day and adopted a new role, cloaking itself mysteriously to successive generations. It is a pity that the date of the Cross can no longer be seen. The late Mr. Crowson assured the writer that, when a young lad, he remembered just making out an incised date on the base. The style, however, is unmistakable and more or less dates itself.

In his travels yours truly discovered several interesting architectural styles in preaching and market crosses. It was at the charming market town of Lavenham that he finally found a cross practically identical to that at March. Were it not for the fact that the shaft well is adorned with badly worn shields and geometric designs, whereas that at Lavenham is plain, the two structures can be likened as twins. Lavenham's example is purely a market cross and according to records it was set up on the old market place in 1501.

Extending his neck the writer makes bold to assert that March Stone Cross was erected by an Order of Friars sometime during the last quarter of the fifteenth century, at about the same time the old church's famous angel roof was installed and a little before the addition of the south porch. Existent for about five hundred years the Stone Cross is much worn and weary with age. One hopes that the powers that be and are yet to come will continue to care for it, that its survival is assured for as long as possible. It is a rare thing, few remaining in the land today.

Long ago a stone monument stood on the Market Place at March. It probably dated from 1670-71 when the market was officially opened on its present site which was ideal for trade brought to the town via the river nearby. The tall, tapering monument known as the Butter Cross served no practical purpose and visually enhanced the main trading area.

MARCH'S OLDEST CARVED STONE

The oldest hand carved object at March can be seen at Saint Wendreda's church in the form of the early Norman font, 1080-1100. The basin, originally square, has eight sides and has crude geometrical incisions which can be interpreted as flower petals or crosses. It stands upon a pedestal dating to the time of the church extension and restoration in the mid fourteenth century. The building was almost entirely rebuilt that it be worthy of receiving the relic of Saint Wendreda previously enshrined within Canterbury cathedral. The angles of the font were erased so as to conform to the octagonal design of the aisle pillars. This ancient font may well signify the existence of a small Norman church at March which presumably replaced a crude Saxon structure of timber framework, mud and reed, perhaps the very one that Wendreda herself had used more than three hundred years previously. On the corner of the font were placed candles, oil and salt to signify respectively Christ Jesus the Light of the world, oil to anoint the body at death depicting the mortality of mankind, and salt the earthiness of men's nature. The water, of course, represented the washing and purifying of the undying spirit. For more than 900 years thousands of babies were brought to this old font which still retains its original lead lining although it is now dry. The font stands just inside the doorway leading to the south porch where can be seen a recessed water stoup. Here the faithful dipped their fingers into the water and made the sign of the cross upon their foreheads before entering the building. In this way it was expected of them to remind themselves of the failings of mankind – as instable as water. The porch witnessed the scenes of women being "churched" after childbirth, then regarded as a necessary ritual before being allowed to enter the church to take part in normal services. Sometimes town officials met there for business.

Walking along West End one observes here and there old cottages and a few old houses which have graced the north bank of the River Nene for more than three hundred years. They are built mainly of brick and during construction of two or three cottages blocks of Barnack stone were incorporated usually at the angles and around door entrances. Looking around a cottage being partly rebuilt the writer was interested to note that the lower walls comprised of seventeenth century bricks with an early nineteenth century upper storey added. The ground floor has several shaped blocks of Barnack stone and it is quite feasible that these may have formed part of an earlier building on the site. It is a fact that stone and other materials were purchased cheaply from the ruination of Thorney abbey and used in the renovation of Saint Wendreda's church in the second half of the sixteenth century. It is probable that secondhand material from the same source was used in the construction and renovation of buildings along West End. Similarly stone and timber was taken from Ramsey abbey and used in the construction of certain colleges at Cambridge where stone from Thorney was welcomed too. It is reasonable to state that smaller amounts of stone, timber, lead and rubble from the great monastic houses were brought to villages and towns in the Fens by boats and by "a man and a boy" as was the case at March.

ANCIENT COFFIN LIDS DISCOVERED

While reading an old book some years ago a piece of paper fell from it onto the writer's lap. A note or two had been written upon it in the mid nineteenth century by Mr. Hamilton of March. He stated that a couple of stone coffin lids served as coping stones on the old wall which almost encompassed Saint Wendreda's church. Anxious to trace these objects, the writer armed hjimself with a fork and prodded around the edges of the churchyard. After searching for several days he was gratified to find at a slight depth two complete stone coffin lids where they had lain for maybe a century or more.

They were placed on the surface where they remain to this day. The lids were hewn in the thirteenth century and one is carved with a pastoral staff. Who rested beneath this old cover? Was the occupant a priest of a church older than the existing building? Or could it have been an abbess or a high ranking person, head of a religious house nearby? From the times of Saint Wendreda March seems to have had connections with a nunnery in the vicinity and the pastoral staffs on the coffin lid would not depict a lay person. The original stone coffin may have been removed from within an older church on the site, the clergy and local dignitaries usually being interred in the nave and aisles. Ordinary people were generally buried in the churchyard, in mediaeval times usually minus a coffin. A body were wrapped in a shroud while the "winding" bell was tolled and a day or two later a communal coffin used to carry it to the church. After a length of time the bones were removed from the soil and reinterred in a communal grave elsewhere in the churchyard to make room for other burials. A sealed lead coffin was discovered in more recent times on the north side of the church. It lies about four feet beneath the surface and is unusually shaped around the body of the corpse. As far as possible mediaeval burials took place on the south and east sides as common superstition associated the devil with the north side where the dark shadow of the steeple creeps along the ground.

Part of another thirteenth century stone coffin lid can be seen within the tower acting as a lintel above a doorway over the spiral stairs. It carries a carving of a florated cross. The tower was built in the latter half of the fourteenth century and given its unusual external passageway in order that the ancient right of way be preserved.

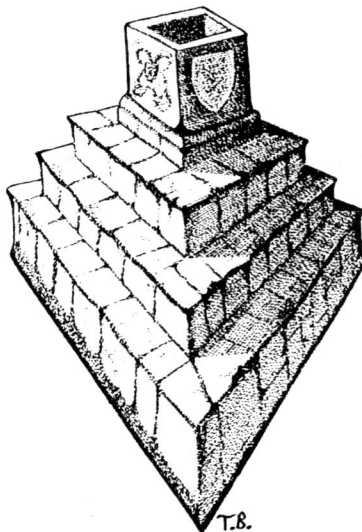

T.B.

They made their mark

FEW PEOPLE born in March have risen to heights of fame. The town has no famous soldiers or bishops, yet in the past certain men made their mark in some particular way and were honoured for achievement in the national interest. The Reverend Christopher Tye was one. Born in the 16th century, Mr. Tye was not a native of the town but he undoubtedly visited the community several times. He was rector of St. Mary's church, Doddington, and as such was automatically in charge of St. Wendreda's church, March which, served by a curate, ranked as a chapelry attached to Doddington.

Christopher Tye is credited as being the father of the English National Anthem, composing the tune used in his day to accompany dancers. A talented musician, he was appointed as Royal organist to the Court of Queen Elizabeth the First. It was not exactly a wise thing to contradict the Queen, but Christopher Tye once did. Listening to him playing the organ on one occasion, her Majesty rebuked Mr. Tye and curtly told him that he was playing out of tune. He promptly retorted that his music was alright and that it was the Queen's ears that were out of tune! But there, he managed to keep his head!

It is not generally known that he gave to the world a tune to accompany a carol which is sung throughout Christendom. At Christmas time men, women and children of all races gather together to sing the beautiful carol "While Shepherds Watched their Flocks by Night" to the lilting notes composed by the Royal organist more than four hundred years ago. It is thrilling to think that the tune to this popular carol may have been heard for the first time in the church at Doddington, yes! and even at March.

MARTIN PIERSON

While on the subject of music, one associates with March a man believed to have first seen the light of day in our little town long ago in the late sixteenth century. He was Martin Pierson, a composer listed in various works of reference although it is difficult to piece together the whole of his life. Born about 1580 he enjoyed a life of considerable activity. He is known to have lived in a house which

29

stood on the site now occupied by "Elwyn House," formerly owned by the late Mr. F. Donald Grounds, adjoining the Market Place. Martin Pierson was doubtless a man of achievement and he became Master of the Choristers of Saint Paul's cathedral.

His name is spelt variously as Pierson, Peirson, Pearson and Peerson. Where he received his early education is not clear, but he graduated Mus. Bac. at Lincoln College, Oxford in 1613. Nine years earlier he came to public notice when he set to music Ben Johnson's words "See, O see who comes here a'maying" which was performed before the King and Queen at Highgate on May Day. This piece was published in his "First Book of Airs and Dialogues" in 1620 – a collection of four, five and six part songs of words and chorus for voices and viols. A second volume, "Motets or Grave Chamber Music," appeared in 1630. Pierson's first patron was the first Lord Brooke Fulke Greville, and, on the latter's death in 1628, the composer wrote a mourning song of six parts.

Pierson was twice married. His first wife was Amy and his second Joanna. On his death he left £100 for the purchase of land, the rent of which was for the provision of "twopenny loaves of good wheaten bread" for between eight and twelve poor persons of the parish of March each Sunday. The land purchased by this donation was Fenhouse Close. He also owned property in Walthamstowe and in the parish of Saint Giles-in-the-Field. Other gifts in his will included sums of money to William Hamos of Sutton Saint Edmunds, Martin Hamos of Saint Ives, Ciceley Dawson of March, his nephews Joseph and Tobias Vickers, and Mary Moulden, in the parish of Christchurch. Mention is also made of a grandson, Antony Holyman.

Biographical details of Martin Pierson are incomplete and there remain a number of interesting questions. Who, for instance, was the Lady Arabella to whom Pierson wrote a funeral ode in 1609? Who was the "right virtuous, beauteous and accomplished Mistress Mary Holder," daughter of the prebendary residential of Southwell to whom he dedicated some of his works?

There is also an interesting local link with the family of Pierson's patron, the first Lord Brooke, for Robert, the second Lord Brooke (1608-1643), a Parliamentary General, relieved Sir Edward Peyton, who was in command of the beseiged Warwick Castle. Robert married Lady Catherine Russell, eldest daughter of Francis, Earl of Bedford, a name for ever associated with the draining of the Fens. Sir Edward was the oldest son of Sir John Peyton, of Isleham, the family having acquired the Manor of Doddington which included March.

It could be that Pierson was connected with Robert Pearson who, from 1607 to 1639 was Rector of North Creake, Norfolk. Possibly he was a brother, for one of Robert's sons was also named Martin, although that could be a coincidence. Robert had two other sons, Richard and John, the latter with a distinguished career. He was Master of Jesus College, Cambridge (1660-62) and Master of Trinity (1662-73). From 1660 to 1673 he was Rector of Terrington and from 1661 to 1672 prebendary of Ely. In 1672 he became Bishop of Chester. He was author and published the well-known "Exposition of the Creed" in 1659.

COUNSELLOR TO KINGS

Another famous name linked with March is that of Sir Antony Hansart, knight, who was appointed High Sheriff of Cambridgeshire, the Isle of Ely and Huntingdon in 1523 and 1529 respectively. This citizen who is commemorated on a brass at Saint Wendreda's church and is honoured in the group of modern residences, Hansart Court, on the Regent site, was elevated to the eminent position of counsellor to Henry the Seventh and Henry the Eighth.

Another March man made his mark in a not too salutory fashion. Robert Wilson stole his father's horse and galloped away from home in the late eighteenth century. Ahead of him lay numerous adventures in foreign lands and he was caught up in numerous mutinees and civil strife. He found himself unwillingly taking part in many dangerous escapades and was accused by foreign governments of spying. More than once he almost lost his life – on one occasion at the hands of head hunters! Fortunately for him he lived a charmed life and managed to wriggle out of trouble and lived to tell the tale. Longing for home he eventually arrived at March to seek his father's forgiveness but he had died only a few week's before. Several townspeople subscribed to his book in which he claimed that he was the world's greatest pedestrian and that no man had travelled on the continents as much as he.

Houseboats and pleasure craft on the River Nene, March, c. 1920.

Town End Fortress

CAVALRY BARN, Battery Fields and Hill Fields are March names with strong military connections. Older residents of the town recall these names, particularly Cavalry Barn which for generations and to this day commemorates a military establishment of centuries ago. Nothing substantial remains of a fortress but there is, however, reasonable evidence in the form of a map preserved at March museum portraying an outline of a military earthwork at March which seems to have been set up at the beginning of the Civil War (c. 1640).

The area in which a fortress is known to have existed lies to the east of Saint Wendreda's church bounded by the new housing development (partly named after a cavalry troop and a Parliamentarian general) and Barkers' Lane. The site of the fortress was almost obliterated by the erection of the Neale-Wade school but a hillock still remains.

Before excavating facts in literal vein, it is prudent in the first instance to acquaint oneself with the importance of the old Isle of Ely constituency, in part renamed Fenland (unfortunately!) during the restive and formative years of the Commonwealth. The Parliamentary cause drew early strength from East Anglia which escaped most of the turmoil and sanguinary effects which are hallmarks of civil strife. This was principally due to the formation of the Eastern Counties' Association with the great Fenman, Oliver Cromwell, at its head. By and large most Isle inhabitants held respect for the Puritan leader although there were at large little pockets of Royalist supporters. Cromwell, as Governor of the Isle of Ely, displayed appropriate feelings for both sides.

Owing to its geographical situation the Isle of Ely, then a vast morass, presented a natural buffer protecting the Eastern Counties' northern flank. The King, too, realised the constituency's strategic importance and at the outset of the war attempted to wrest the Isle from the forces which sought to overthrow him. The Isle of Ely formed a passage into the very heart of the malignant Association. Fen soldiers, rough-clad pioneers of what was soon to become England's invincible Model Army, the envy of military commanders in Europe, stood their ground and prevented the Cavaliers from gaining ground. The enemy was flushed out at King's Lynn and Crowland and the Isle was never subjected to the test again.

For most part the Isle proved loyal to Parliament, although that may be measured in terms of indifference. Anxious moments did arise, certain Royalist sympathisers testing reaction by creating disturbances at Ely where Cromwell had lived for ten years as collector of the tithes. He was never forgiven for closing the cathedral for a decade or more. The faction of Royalist exponents at Wisbech could not be let out of sight either. Overtures of war rose to a crescendo and with the King's armies gaining early advantages the Isle of Ely was placed on full alert.

Colonel Fairfax, Parliamentary Commander of Colchester Garrison entertained grave doubts about the security of the Isle and advised that everything be done to fortify the area. Accordingly a troop of sixty horse placed under the command of Colonel John Hobart of Outwell were sent to the Isle and regularly patrolled the area. The Isle inhabitants were taxed to the tune of £70 per week to maintain the troop. Another troop emplacement was situated west of Wisbech to watch over the fen from the Crowland direction.

Cromwell who, it was said, had been heard to declare his intention of making the Isle of Ely "a fit place for God to dwell," frequently visited the area in the early days of the war. At least on one occasion he stayed near Wisbech. An elderly man of Elm in 1827 remembered his grandfather remark that, as a young boy, he had watched Cromwell pass through the avenue leading to Needham Hall. There the owner made him and his troops welcome and Cromwell, so as to be not more comfortable than his men, slept on a table while the escort party made themselves as comfortable as possible in adjoining outbuildings.

Not surprisingly, Wisbech, enjoying as it did, status as a Borough by Royal Charter, seems to have had more than a passing interest in the fortunes and misfortunes of the King. The town's Royalists, gathering in secret, would place bread crumbs in wine and give a toast with a double meaning: "May Providence send this crumb well (Cromwell) down!." Wisbech was a trifling thorn in Parliament's armoured side and the Royalist sympathisers were closcly marked. When the Isle was threatened by Cavaliers who approached the Fens through south Lincolnshire, Colonel Watson in overall command of the northern part of the Isle, began to disarm suspected and known opponents and "arm honest men if they be found."

The Marquis of Newcastle for King Charles drew near with a large army and Captain Dobson of the Isle's defence forces, rated as a highly capable officer of utmost severity and discipline, rounded up

Wisbech's reactionaries and interred them in the commodious parish church until the crisis had passed. The Cavaliers were deflected from the northern flanks and Parliament strengthened its strategic positions.

DISPLAYED THE FLAG AT MARCH

At this point readers may ask where March came into the picture. Two things should be borne in mind: *(a)* March was strategically placed in the Isle of Ely and in the southern Fens in particular; *(b)* it is known that the old time constituency was regularly patrolled by a Parliamentarian cavalry troop which displayed the flag and rigorously enforced security.

Both Ely and Wisbech had military personnel within their respective boundaries. When considering the then inconvenient location of these two principal towns – one far north, and the other in the south of the Isle – it was unlikely that the troop of horse had its headquarters at either of those places. Rather the troop was stationed at a central town for greater convenience and expediency of enforcing martial law in all directions. The protrusion upon which the town of March is situated, the second largest "island" in the Fens, offered an ideal point from which to centralise security operations. March was conveniently placed upon the Fen causeway and commanded approaches to the island from virtually every direction. It was also near Chatteris situated at the north end of Ireton's Way, known locally as the Mepal Straight, a long stretch of road towards the high prominence of land on which is situated the City of Ely. This road was driven through the wet fens by order of General Ireton mainly for military purposes.

At no place in the former Isle of Ely is "cavalry" referred to in any sense relating to a military establishment other than at March. When hurriedly setting up military posts it was often necessary to commandeer suitable buildings overlooking an open area which would lend itself to defensive and counter offensive actions. It was a recognised policy during the Civil War for both sides to requisition suitable buildings and, if deemed desirable, erect timber pallisades and earth mounds on which to mount cannon. Examples of this type of make-shift fortress is evidenced in the numerous pallisaded outposts erected in the nineteenth century by the Federal and Union forces of America in the epic struggle of the Civil War. At March, "Cavalry Barn," "Battery Hills" and Field Baulk present positive clues. The word cavalry explains itself; battery indicates cannon; and baulk refers to an earthwork as does "hills." As a teenager the writer remembers walking across the fields from Eastwood Avenue to Barkers Lane and observing odd ground irregularities in the form of mounds and earthworks as well as large blocks of stone half buried in the soil. Older residents were well familiar with the earth ridge and ditches, which I think had formed a rectangular moat in a grassed area known as Hills Field.

NOT A ROYALIST STRONGHOLD

If readers had lived in the nineteenth century they would have seen a great deal more of these hills of mystery. One might even have met the adventurous Captain Hamilton who, in the summer of 1849, made excavations on the site and revealed ample evidence of a fortress of some kind. The so-called hills were, in fact, circular mounds; one, at the time seemed to be in a reasonable state. Captain Hamilton also exposed remains of a timber pallisade. That evidence together with the visible earthworks, and bearing in mind the plan kept in March

CIVIL WAR EARTHWORK
MARCH • circa 1640

Later alterations ?
House or Barn ?
Gun emplacement
Gun emplacement

Ground plan of Civil War fortress at March. Much of the earthwork dating to c. 1640 was filled in during 1939-45. It is supposed that it was used by a Parliamentary troop, possibly of horse.

35

Museum clearly defines the outline of a fortress having its main front towards the north and with circular mounds on which presumably cannons were mounted. The remains of the moat lay on the south side. It was about twenty feet wide. Furthermore, the interior of the site contained foundations of "a large building."

The west and north walls of this edifice comprised of large stone blocks and the east and south walls were brick. According to Captain Hamilton the main entrance was gained by crossing a drawbridge over the fosse, and remains of a road led directly from the earthworks to Saint Wendreda's church. This road is probably the existing Barker's Lane. The discovery in the ruin of pottery and tobacco pipes of the time of the Commonwealth strengthens the supposition that a building here had been requisitioned and defensive additions added by soldiers under Cromwell's command.

Church towers made excellent observation posts and both Ironsides and Cavaliers were known to use them. At March the church was conveniently near. As was the custom in those troublesome times one imagines that at least one soldier attended church services. Practically all the Isle's clergy were Royalist sympathisers. Puritan soldiers were usually detailed to attend services, the "Souldier's Bible" resting on one knee and his sword upon the other knee to encourage clergy to preach strongly but simply and discourage attempts to enlist mens hearts to the King's cause.

Early this century, the author of *"Records of a Fen Parish"* commented briefly on the earthworks at March, and suggested that they had been manned for the King. This, in the writer's view, was highly unlikely. While there is every reason to believe that the mounds did serve as gun emplacements, there is no doubt that the gun battery kept there was installed by Parliamentary troops to defend the premises which one venture's to assume formed the headquarters of a cavalry unit whose duty it was to quell uprisings as well as guard the causeway from the centre of the Isle to Ely.

Despite disturbances at Ely and the pro-Royalist attitudes of not a few Wisbechians at the time, not once through military brandishment did these factions pose a serious threat to Cromwell's hold on the Isle of Ely. That the gun emplacements at March were held for King Charles is a fallacy. If that had been possible the battery and its crew would have been swiftly dealt with in this, the northern bulwark of Mr. Cromwell's masterful force. The Ironsides were firmly in control of the area, although many young men from our fair fenny island were known to have enlisted more or less equally on both sides and were engaged in terrible battles elsewhere in the country. It is an interesting point that at March it seems that a substantial building stood within the earthworks. Timber pallisades were hastily erected on a temporary basis. Numerous manor houses were seized and fortified by the opposing armies, churches too, as happened at Crowland. On the face of it, it seems that the military requisitioned an existing building and converted it into a fortress-cum-store.

In his notes Captain Hamilton suggested that this building could have been a crenellated mansion. Perhaps it was a tithe barn? After all we have Cavalry Barn. Then again, would a moat be excavated around a barn? Mediaeval manors were designed as comfortable and spacious homes and did, in fact, preserve the castellan's impressive, traditional embellishments of moat and crenellated parapets as a token means of defence. But the emphasis was almost entirely cosmetic. Crenellated buildings and moats had become outdated and in the hey-day of powder and ball these were not features in seventeenth century military design. It seems that March had a second fortress near the present by-pass. Earthworks were thrown up to enclose a large rectangular area along Burrowmoor Road which passes through the actual site. It would make sense to have a military presence there, as the track represented another entrance from the west onto the island.

An interesting question arises: Could the "large building" within the earthworks on the Neale Wade site be the original Eastwood Manor? One may never know, but this much is certain. March clearly played a part in the momentous event of the Civil War and the establishment of the Commonwealth.

The Jubilee Fountain is one of a few. Its "fenny" emblems make it unique.

37

Nineteenth Century March

NINETEENTH CENTURY March was well known over a wide area for garden produce, much of it grown along the riverside and in the vicinity of Burrowmoor Road, Deerfield and Badgeney. The town had no fewer than ten professional gardeners and seedsmen in 1825. Flowers also played a notable part in the gardeners' seasonal tasks.

The curates of March formerly resided at a Georgian house in High Street. There they derived inspiration from one-and-a-half acres of surrounding garden land. In 1836 a Mr. Fuller expended not an inconsiderable amount of time, energy and money laying out exquisite floral displays on this extensive piece of ground in the vicinity of The Maze. On it he planted various flowering plants of choice quality, including American varieties and evergreens; all combined to provide the town centre with an agreeably attractive showpiece. The exotic gardens as they were known were the delight of local people and were patronised by visitors from places several miles away.

ELEVEN SCHOOLS AT MARCH

In the nineteenth century March was well provided for in fields of education. The century was one of revelation and revolution and it was quickly realised that if the country was to become a world leader, emphasis must be placed on suitable means of educating the young. Education on an organised and disciplined basis was needful; it was also good business. Practically every town in the country offered competitive educational facilities and several with populations of approximately five thousand boasted a dozen educational establishments. Compare the population and schools of Fen towns at the time of the census in 1821: Chatteris had six schools and academies to serve a population of 3,283; Ely (10), 5,079; Upwell/Outwell/Manea (7) 4,236; Whittlesey (11), 5,276; Wisbech (22) 7,877.

In that decade the young people of March dragged themselves snail-like to no less than eleven schools. There was built in 1827 a large winged edifice which served, in part, as the Guildhall where elected individuals served the town's interests, or were supposed to! In it were held manorial courts and a court of requests. It also served as schools accommodated in two spacious wings and run under the National System. In 1850 the average number of boys daily attending was one-hundred-and-seventy, but during winter the figure fell to about seventy. On an average girls totalled seventy throughout the seasons. The headmaster received a salary of £100 a year and the schoolmistress £50. Boys were instructed in reading, writing, grammar, history, drawing, mental arithmetic, the use of globes, geography, natural history, the phonic system of reading, Hullah's system of singing, and exercises in arithmetic after the method of Pestalozzi, etc., etc. All good stuff! The shool was well equipped with maps, pictorial drawings, tablets, books and blackboards. Oh yes, and canes as well to make sure pupils paid attention.

The town's oldest educational institution, the Grammar School, was an able competitor and specialised in academic studies. It was founded at the end of the 17th century and, with the town's secondary schools, was absorbed into the debatable Comprehensive system. Nowadays, March, with a population (1993) of between 16,000 and 17,000 accommodates its scholars and some from outlying areas, in half-a-dozen schools.

In 1830 most schools at March were run by private individuals, some of whom were ambitious "lecturers." Proprietor/teachers were: Mary Cave, High Street; Ann and Emma Elliott (day and boarding), High Street; Benjamin Green, Whittle End; Azubah Harrison, Stone Cross House; Jane and Mary Jarrums, Well End; Elizabeth Lane, High Street; Walter Michaux, Well End; and George Pierce, Town End, had his school at the existing church room attached to Saint Wendreda's. Parents paid for their children's education. Adults, too, had their chance to learn in what was then a largely illiterate society, Hewitt Clark's enterprise catering solely for adult males.

In addition to this latter-mentioned amenity the adult population availed itself of the opportunities in the curriculum offered at the Mechanic's Institute, its site now occupied by the Nat-West bank in Broad Street. The old step-gabled building was sometimes used as a theatre. The Institute was founded on October 3rd, 1845 and had three rooms, one for reading. another for lectures and a third for use of committees. For practical reasons all three rooms could be thrown into one. This worthwhile institution was formed to instruct members, especially the working class, in various branches of science connected with their respective vocations, and also to enlighten the prying mind anxious to learn of developments in the world. It promoted general and useful knowledge in arranging classes and had a museum, a circulating library, a discussion group and invited popular lecturers to address the members.

The Institute was sustained by payment of two shillings half-yearly or four shillings in advance per member, holders of ordinary subscriptions enjoying all benefits. Members subscribing ten shillings per annum were entitled to attend lectures and discussions and could visit the museum. Those that could afford one pound enjoyed the privilege of introducing a friend to any of the functions. A gift of five pounds or more made the donor a member for life. Likewise if a member presented books or apparatus to the value of eight pounds. The early Victorian age introduced a great thirst for knowledge, and the working man who had suffered suppression for so long at the hands of the titled gentry, notably land owners, had at last a chance to benefit from the new age of opportunity. Yet there were those

Olde time window display in High Street.

40

that keenly opposed advances aimed at the edification of the working class, led by the likes of Prime Minister Robert Peel and a host of judicary officials. It were people such as the Duke of Bedford who farmed a large estate at Thorney, twelve miles from March, who forced the issue and made the life of a working man far more tolerable. Apart from fresh water the Duke provided the rare privilege of education for his workforce and their families. Someone at March had a similar, if limited vision as well.

THE LONG DISTANCE RUNNER

In old times transport never came easy in the Fens, except possibly by water and that not always to be desired. Fen roads were constantly in a deplorable state, deeply pitted and furrowed. It was the practice of councils to hire farmers to plough and roll the country lanes to make them more passable. Even the towns, like March, had bad roads although the main highways were usually metalled. In winter lesser roads were nothing less than quagmires and contributed to terrible living conditions and diseases of the most serious order as was the unfortunate case of our own little town.

This state of affairs reflected well into the twentieth century. No-one travelled unless they were obliged to and it was sometimes less hazardous to journey by river rather than road. John Smith's passenger/luggage boat service plied between March and Cambridge once a fortnight in 1825, and the enterprising waterman used his craft to take March folk to King's Lynn market once a week.

Carriers were extremely busy men. Day and Company's "Waggon" departed from the White Hart on Mondays and Thursdays at 6 a.m. destined for Saint Ives, Cambridge and London. Gilby and Wallaces' team strained at their halters to start the waggon from The Chequers every Wednesday and Saturday evening, headed in the same direction. Brighton's cart left the White Lion for Downham Market on Wednesdays.

The lonely, exposed road to Whittlesey clattered to the rythmic pitch of John Robert's team from the White Hart on Mondays and Fridays. He vied for custom with another runner from the Chequers. Day and Co's. vehicle dragged away from the White Hart on Mondays and Fridays en route for Wisbech, via Elm and Friday Bridge. He also had competition from Gilby and Wallis (Chequers), and Thomas Hutchison and William Watson, all of whom took a share of this lucrative route.

A sharp toot-toot from a coachman's horn announced the approach of the stagecoach. There was nothing more dramatic to set a small boy's dreams a-flying than the arrival of the stagecoach, steaming pairs and fours clip-clopping and slithering to a halt in the cobbled yard of the Griffin Inn. The arrival of a long distance runner always evoked interest among the locals. Had the coach escaped the attention of highwaymen? Who was it carrying? Someone famous, perhaps? A long-lost relative? The long-coated reinsman oozed importance and the guard with his horn had discreetly hidden a blunderbus. Passengers descended from the dust-covered vehicle and made haste into the yard where, on cold days, they warmed themselves before a log fire and regaled in the good old English tradition. Porters emptied the boot of luggage and stable lads took charge of and watered the animals.

March regularly witnessed the arrival and departure of the "Day" and the "Defiance." The "Day" from Wisbech called at the Griffin every Monday, Wednesday and Friday at 8 a.m., and the "Defiance" drew to a halt in the inn yard on Tuesdays, Thursdays and Saturdays at the same hour. According to an old plan they probably entered the yard through a passageway at the front of the building. Both coaches left March bound for London via Cambridge, Wadesmill and Ware. They called at the Griffin on the return journey.

195 TRADERS AT MARCH IN 1825

The list of traders and professional residents is based on a directory of about 1825. Local traders in that period valued the custom of the gentry. Whereas the poorer classes had little in the way of cash to spare and purchased only items of necessity, ladies and gentlemen of means enjoyed luxuries aplenty and their larders and wardrobes were usually filled to overflowing. It was considered quite out of order to appear socially in clothes worn previously at similar functions. Well, the ladies thought that way. Things haven't changed all that much! The gentry's additional spending habits with local traders nonetheless played an important role in the stability of local economy, and the well-to-do were gratified to see their names in the county directory. It was a kind of mutual, if not patronising, custom. Certainly to blaze one's name for free was good for business.

When comparing the various trades of the 1820's, change in manufacture and demand is readily visible. Several old trades have vanished in the wake of scientific and industrial progress and changing demands as befits modern society. The list of local manufacturers illustrates what was once the hub of our town and its economic existence. All these crafts had a viable and purposeful place in the day to day life of nineteenth century March: Basket makers, sieve makers, boot and shoe makers (quite different to the friendly cobbler), brick makers, coopers, glovers, lime burners, maltsters, millwrights, rope and twine makers, straw hat makers, tallow chandlers, wheelwrights, whitesmiths, fellmongers, brassfounders, staymakers, braziers, gilders. Many items were made to order, for instance, boots and shoes, hats and gloves. Mass manufacturing and convenient means of payment had not yet materialised and would not do so until the wage structure had changed. Local manufacturers were their own retailers and some private residences even combined factory and shop.

Mainly due to the cogwheel evolution and introduction of steam power the majority of old crafts succumbed. Much the same as we are experiencing in modern times when the computer has, in fact, eliminated the need of many hands. It's a similar story. As in the eighteen hundreds revolutionary methods of manufacture, while enhancing the earnings of the privileged directly threatens the livelihood of the underprivileged. It has always been so.

It is appropriate to try and envisage March of one-hundred-and-seventy years ago with its motley and irregular assortment of thatched, slated and pantiled houses, cottages and trading premises. In High Street there were 111 trading premises; Well End (Nene Parade) 20; Bridge Street (Broad Street) 20; Whittle End (West End) 18; the Market Place 6; Sumps (off High Street) 6; Town End 6; Stone Cross 2; Bellmetal Lane 1; Brooks Lane 1; Wisbech Road 1; Church End 1; Norwood Side 1; High Dyke (the Hythe area west of High Street) 1. Traders catered for the needs of approximately 5,000 inhabitants.

March was thirsty, too! Nineteen taverns and a couple of inns slaked parched throats: Anchor (Garner Oliver) Well End; Black Swan (Edward Dring) Whittle End; Boot and Shoe (George Freear) Whittle End; Bushel (Whenham Powers) Sumps; Carpenters Arms (James Proudfoot) Sumps (this tavern stood on the site of the car park adjacent to the park, it also accommodated tramps; Chequers (William Manning) Bridge Street; The Cock (Matthew Beckerton) High Street;

Crown (William Jaggard) Well End; The George (Joseph Hudson) High Street; Green Man (Edred Everson) High Street; The Plough (Rebecca Lewis) Sumps; Red Hart (Ann Rhodes) High Street; Red Lion (William Bains) High Street; Seven Stars (John Swan) Town End; Shoulder of Mutton (Joseph Hudson) High Street; Three Fishes (John Ogden) Whittle End; The Wheel (Thomas Freear) Bridge Street, this tavern stood opposite the Fountain; White Horse (Robert Bridges) Whittle End; White Lion (Thomas Christmas) High Street, junction of Saint Peter's Road then called White Lion Lane; The Griffin Inn (John Iliffe) High Street, staging house traced at least to the seventeenth century; White Hart Inn (William Kirkham) adjacent to the bridge, Bridge Street. The Ship Inn, Nene Parade was not listed, presumably as it was then a shop or a private residence.

MARCH PROFESSIONS AND BUSINESSES
circa 1825

ATTORNEYS (3) – Daniel Barley, Edmund Barley, Matthew Richard.

AUCTIONEERS AND APPRAISERS (3) – Barley & Elliott, John Pope, William Pratt & Son.

BAKERS AND FLOUR DEALERS (10) – Edward Booth, Thomas Booth, John Campbell, John Elliott, John Fletcher, Isaac Lee, John Peake, Thomas Pope, William Shearhod (also fruiterer), Matthew Southwell.

BANKERS (1) – Gurneys, Birkbeck and Peckover (branch of Wisbech bank).

BASKET AND SIEVE MAKERS (2) – Isaac Freeman, William White.

BLACKSMITHS (6) – Susan Barley, Charles Bates, Stephen Butcher, Charles Dobson, Joseph Hopper, William Pooley.

BOOKSELLERS, STATIONERS AND BINDERS (3) – Matthew Edward Croft (also printer and paper hanger), Thomas Sargent, Thomas Withnoe (also printer and stationer).

BOOT AND SHOE MAKERS (8) – Sarah Beeby, Thomas Camps, William Golding, John Goodson, Isaac Jervis, John Johnson, Thomas Watson, Thomas Wigston.

BREWERS (4) – Nathan Gray (ale and porter), Thomas Phillips (retail), William Pope, John Thurbon (retail).

BRICKMAKERS (3) – Thomas Orton, Thomas Phillips, John Woodward.

BUILDERS (10, including bricklayers and joiners) – William Beeton, John Bodger, Robert Graves, William Hutchinson, John Johnson, Thomas Phillips (and stone and marble mason), James Searle, Anthony Setchfield, William Shearhod, Matthew Smith.

BUTCHERS (8) – Robert Brighty, Robert Chapman, Thomas Christmas, Mary Dobson, George Freear, Jonathan Sherhod, John Wadlow, John Walters.

CARPENTERS AND JOINERS (4) – Thomas Bell, Robert Graves (also cabinet maker), Joseph Layton, Daniel Ruff.

CHINA AND GLASS DEALERS (3) – Miles Peggs, Thomas Pope, Charles Simmons.

CHYMISTS AND DRUGGISTS (3) – William Bevill, Thomas Dawbarn & Co., Henry Pope.

CLOTHES DEALERS (2) – Sarah Beeby, Thomas Roberts.

COOPERS (3) – Robert Chapman, John Tunnel, William Wright.

CORN AND COAL MERCHANTS (5) – Thomas Booth (coal), Thomas Elliott (corn), Thomas Phillips (coal), Smith & Cole (corn), John Smith (coal).

FIRE AND OFFICE AGENTS (7) – "Atlas": John Andrews & Co., "British & Commercial": William Booth, "Herts & Cambridgeshire": John Pope, "Norwich Union": John Thurbon, "Protector": William Booth, "Royal Exchange": Edward Elam, "Suffolk & General Country": John Smith.

FISHMONGERS (3) – Benjamin Buxton, Ann Rhodes, Richard Wright.

GARDENERS AND SEEDSMEN (10) – Robert Chapman, Thomas Cornwell, Edred Everson, John Halliday, David Head, Stephen Read, Ann Rhodes, Robert James (also fruit), John Smith, John Stratton.

GLOVERS (2) – Robert Graves, Charles Smith.

GROCERS, TEA DEALERS AND DRAPERS (8) – John Andrew & Co. (also hatters), William Booth, Thomas Dawbarn & Co. (also hatters), Edward Elam, John Partridge, Henry Pope (grocer), John Smith, John Thurbon.

HAIR DRESSERS (2) – Robert Graves, Charles Smith.

IRONMONGERS (2) – Charles Bates, Sarah Beedzler.

LIME BURNERS (2) – Thomas Phillips, John Smith.

MALTSTERS (2) – Nathan Gray, John Smith.

MILLERS (4) – Thomas Boon, Samuel Green, Edward Harewood, Edward Matthews.

MILLINERS AND DRESS MAKERS (7) – Jane Burton, Rebecca and Mary English, Susannah Miller, Francis Ogden, Mary Powers, Elizabeth Redhead, Lucy White.

MILLWRIGHTS (7) – William Beeton jun., John Bodger, Robert Graves, Joseph Pope, Daniel Ruff, William Shearhod, Matthew Smith.

PAINTERS, PLUMBERS AND GLAZIERS (3) – Owen Gray, William Smith, James Woodstock.

ROPE AND TWINE MAKERS (2) – Lewis Amos, William Nightingale.

SADDLERS AND COLLAR MAKERS (3) – Lewis Amos, James Band, Merchant Coy.

SHOPKEEPERS AND DEALERS IN SUNDRIES (5) – John Barker, Robert Chapman, Rebecca English, Daniel Leach, Miles Peggs.

STRAW HAT MAKERS (5) – Mary Goodson, Mary Layton, Francis Ogden, Caroline Olivier, Mary Ann Sarjent.

SURGEONS (3) – John Church, Charles Culledge, William Hawyes Wray.

SURVEYORS (4) – Joseph Jackson (of land, also land agent), Thomas Ogden (road), John Partridge (land), William Pratt & Son (of roads, also land agent)

TAILORS (10) – Thomas Abbott, Lowder Burrows, Robert Burrows, William Gray, William Jaggard, Thomas Roberts (also draper), John Smith (also draper), John Smith jun., Joseph Southwell (also draper), William Yarrow.

TALLOW CHANDLER (1) – Thomas Scargell.

WATCH AND CLOCK MAKERS (2) – George Smith, John Smith.

WHEELWRIGHTS (5) – Thomas Cunnington, Joseph Pope (also joiner), William Shearhod (also joiner), Charles Simmons, William Simmons.

WHITESMITHS (3) – David Ballard, Robert Glascock, Robert Miller.

WINE AND SPIRIT MERCHANTS (5) – William Bevill (spirit), Thomas Dawbarn & Co. (British wine), Nathan Gray (spirit and porter), John Pope sen. (spirit), William Pope (wine and porter).

MISCELLANEOUS – George Ball, fellmonger; Ann Britchford, flour dealer; Charles Cross, boat builder; Emerson Harrison Friend, veterinary surgeon; Robert Glascock, brass founder; John Partridge, parish clerk; William Pratt sen., coroner for the Isle of Ely; Eliza Smith, staymaker; John Todd, Governor of Eastwood workhouse; Joseph West, carver and gilder; John and Samuel Smith, timber and iron merchants; Samuel Smith, merchanist; William Towler, brazier and tin plate worker; William White, upholsterer; Thomas Withnoe sen., clerk of court of requests.

It will be noticed that certain skilled traders of March had dual and triple busnesses. They carried out their work at a time when most inhabitants still recalled with pride the defeat of Napoleon Bonaparte at Waterloo. The bellringers at Saint Wendreda's church especially so, for they had rung a peal of 5,040 changes on the bells to celebrate the victory. Inhabitants viewed with growing trepidation rumours that the Fens' wind engines were to be replaced with powerful steam pumps to vanquish the last remnants of water and marsh in the outlying areas. Little did they know that gas fuel and the railway (what memories March has of that) were barely twenty years away.

By the way, did you spot any ancestors?

The Griffin "Fly" waiting for custom at March Station.

Economy of a small Fen town

OVER THE course of eleven centuries the Fen economy was based mainly on food such as fish, wildfowl, beast, sheep, swine and on material from trees such as alder and willow and, of course, reed. The inhabitants, sometimes known as Beezlings and Girvii (men of the marsh), rarely ventured onto the uplands overlooking the Fens. They had no need to. Fish and fowl were very popular in the cities as well as among the Fen people and were so abundant as to make the inhabitants more or less independent of the rest of the world at large. Horses reared in the Fens were recognised for strength and durability and were reared for the army. Masses of reed were sold to people living beyond the Fens who sometimes exchanged earthenware goods for Fen material. Crops of wheat were abundant on the Fen islands, and the lower level after wintry inundation excelled in grazing for sheep and cattle.

The men of March enjoyed gainful employment at the fisheries and were skilled at wildfowling. A Fenman was capable of catching wild duck in flight with a looped pole, and his punt gun could take out at least twelve dozen fowl with a single shot. The commons on Norwoodside and Lynwood were ideal grazing ground for cattle and other livestock and the beech woods provided shelter and food for hogs.

The old time Fenman was not inclined to be sociable and visitors were viewed with suspicion, attitudes which arose because strangers tried to interfere with the Fenmen's birthright. But the Fen dweller more than matched the upland citizens with cunning and patience, minded his own business and left no-one in any doubt as to where he stood. The environment which suited him and his neighbours was abhorred by "hillmen." Time had set his hand and Fenmen met their match with the coming of the drainage undertakers spurred on by visions of capital gain. *(Water, Water Everywhere - T. Bevis).*

Thousands of acres of fen were purchased and after numerous setbacks through shortsightedness and ill-conceived planning, a new era of Fen economy emerged. The area became a Klondyke of "black gold" and whole new communities were established to work the fields on which two and even three crops could be grown in one season. Fenman who had suffered hard times during drainage attempts at last enjoyed the prospects of full employment, thousands of acres of former wet land emerging for the attention of wealthy speculators. The farmers tended to live in the townships but later moved to the outlying fen for greater convenience. They built several elegant houses at March and some display the opulence of the Georgian era.

Thus March began another stage in its expansion and a bright new dawn shone above the town. Boats, nets and eel traps were put away and replaced with spades, hoes, harrows and ploughshares. The promise made by the drainage undertakers had, after a couple of centuries, become reality. It was not always necessary to use the plough and the fine soil was constantly rolled. Crops could be grown without so much as a farrow and young plants grew so vigorously that women and children were employed to trample upon the shoots to delay growth. It was no coincidence that the Fens became known nationally as The Nation's Larder and The Breadbasket of England.

The good fortune of our market town was further enhanced with the coming of the railway in 1846 and later development of Whitemoor railway marshalling yards, thanks to the shortsightedness of eminent Wisbech banker, Lord Peckover, who imposed unacceptable conditions upon the railway company on enquiry as to the possibility of developing the centre on land at Wisbech. The company then favoured March, and the railway from its centralised position in turn encouraged the establishment of the County Hall at March which became the county town of the former Isle of Ely. The railway was the ecomical factor behind major development within the town.

EARNED A SHILLING A DAY

Serious expansion at March can be traced from the end of the sixteenth century when the population stood at approximately 1,000 (based on eligible communicants). There was little room to expand in the centre which can be broadly defined as High Street and Bridge Green (Broad Street), the riverside and Badgeney areas. The town was hemmed in by extensive commons managed by fenreves and generally used for the grazing of livestock. As few areas could be built upon, young couples began to encroach upon the commons. They set up homes and were fined lightly, but a precedent had been made and families were allowed to stay. Most commonable residences were built of lath and plaster and covered with reed thatch. Bricks were too expensive for ordinary people. At the end of the seventeenth century Maximilian Walsham's kiln at March produced bricks sold at £1 per hundred. Thatch was 15s. for six hundred of reed and the thatcher received 17s. 6d. for a week's work. Labourers took home less than a shilling a day and a skilled hedger 11s. 8d. for two weeks' work. The eighteenth century did not add significantly to the town's population, the district economy suppressed by land drainage works and numerous problems still arose from winter flooding. Several families employed in the old fen-related trades as well as a number of disappointed farmers left the area and sought better luck in the upland regions.

At the beginning of the 19th century the population of March had reached about 2,500. In 1831 this had changed to 5,147 and despite a spate of cholera and typhoid outbreaks, etc., in 1841 5,706 people lived in the town. Eighteen-forty-nine proved an inglorious year for March during which it earned the unfortunate reputation of having the highest mortality rate per head of population in the country. The population then stood at 6,300 and there were 1,215 dwellings, many more aptly described as hovels with shared toilets. They accommodated amidst indescribable squalor 986 paupers while the remainder of North Witchford had no more than 1,100 such cases. It was many years before March fully recovered. After the town had been cleansed and piped water laid on to every house and cottage, its future as an agricultural based community was assured. The County Hall stamped its presence on Cambridgeshire and the Isle of Ely and March became a byword throughout the railway system of Britain. In terms of population March overtook Whittlesey, Ely and Chatteris and by 1911 enjoyed a count of 8,403 heads. Thirty years' later this had increased to 12,993. While committing pen to paper the number of people living at March is more or less 17,000. It is conceivable that a population of 20,000 is within the town's capability but, bearing in mind the unique rural environment with its strong agricultural influence, a population in excess of that conjectured figure to my mind seems undesirable. It is a known fact that communities with large populations experience attendant problems and their economies are not necessarily improved. As this is being written a severe recession affects the country and the world at large. March has been fortunate in that it has managed to attract to its acres more industry than ever before and, with the demise of the railway marshalling yards, the shortfall is partly made up with the setting up of H.M. Prison Whitemoor with a staff of several hundred.

Norwood Road windmill.

Windmills of the mind

W INDMILLS and other types of mills at March exist only in the mind, that is they are but memories. It cannot be established whether March had a mill or mills before the reign of Queen Elizabeth the First. Doddington had one in 1250 and that may have served Merc which was then a "fair sized village" and a part of the Manor of Doddington in any case. Our town might well have had a mill or two in the 14th century, but a post-mill is clearly shown standing on Norwood Common on an Elizabethan map of Fenland waterways published about 1580.

A wind engine, like a windmill but with a water scoop, stood at the bottom of Gaul Road. Like a great many other water devices it was probably erected sometime in the latter half of the 17th century to drain water from reclaimed fen into the River Nene. This, however, was not designed to grind corn. Its successor is a diesel driven unit. A windmill for grinding corn displayed elegant sails at the top end of Gaul Road. It was erected in the 18th century, the writer having seen accounts from a book written during that century by an ancestor of the late Mr. S. Billitt who owned the site. This mill was eventually dismantled and replaced with new buildings containing a power plant.

A post windmill must have stood on Lynwood common between Wimblington and March. It could have been erected in the 17th century as one does not show on the ancient waterway map, but is commemorated in Mill Hill Lane and Mill Hill Drove. Another mill stood in the vicinity of the entrance from Station Road to Creek Road. A tunnel is associated with this old mill, although is it more likely to have been connected with a brewery nearby. The vaulted tunnel leading to the river was discovered in the vicinity of the Ship Inn. Barges drew up by a wooden wharf and loaded and unloaded materials beneath Nene Parade to and from the brewery – or the mill – with no inconvenience to nearby inhabitants and pedestrians.

An exceptionally fine looking brick windmill stood on the south side of Burrowmoor Road. Another with sails turning gently in the breeze could be found in Smith's Close, off Norwood Road. By far the most important of March mills was erected in the nineteenth century a short distance from Acre Wharf, near the town bridge. The building which originally stood on the site, owned by Owen Gray, served for several years as a warehouse for coal, turf, grain and timber, exported via the waterways to other communities in the Fens and beyond. A Mr. Smith bought the premises and he enlarged the complex and installed a fine steam engine to power the mill. Produce was distributed to all parts of the country. At one time the building was temporarily used by a theatrical company as well as by the Independents, a religious denomination.

Other mills of March which were closed in more recent times were Mortons Mill, Station Road, the site occupied by a block of flats, and Smith's Mill in High Street, later sold to Lloyds Engineers.

Threshing operations near March.

Burrowmoor Road windmill.

MARCH THROUGH THE AGES – IN BRIEF

3rd CENTURY – Large Roman settlement with signs of flooding.

7th CENTURY, late/early 8th CENTURY – Wendreda at Merc.

9th CENTURY – Translation of Saint Wendreda's mortal remains to Ely monastery.

c. 1000 – Merc given to Ely monastery by Oswy and Leofleda when their son became a monk.

1086 (Domesday Survey) – Merc part of the Manor of Doddington. 12 villeins each working 12 acres of land.

1249 – 12 acres of marsh in Merche granted by Bishop Northwold to St. Neots priory.

1251 – Merche "a fair sized village" with 77 messuages. River area known as Mercheford. There were 35 free and about 50 servile tenants. Church enlarged(?).

1328 – A manor (Hatchwood) mentioned for the first time.

1343 – Indulgence granted by Pope Clement VI on the building (or rebuilding) of the church. Translation of Saint Wendreda's relic from Canterbury to March.

1360/1380 – Tower added to church.

1450 – March possessed seven gilds.

1480–1526 – Double hammerbeam angel roof installed at Saint Wendreda's church to commemorate saint enshrined there.

1480–1500 – Wayside cross set up along The Causeway.

c. 1546 – Shrine dismantled and religious figures and emblems, etc., removed from church.

1566 – March classed as a minor port with eight boats carrying, one, one-and-a-half or two cartloads of coal and grain.

1596 – A school mentioned at March.

1640–45 – Civil War: Fortress erected at Town End.

1671 – Market established with two annual fairs.

1699 – A town hall at March.

1700 – Baptist cause officially established at March. A congregation met before that year in private premises.

1730 – Three urns filled with burnt bones and a pot containing 160 Roman *denarii* discovered in Robin Goodfellows Lane.

1793 – Post office established.

1798 – Six Anglican and one nonconformist schools at March.
1799 – Baptist church built (rebuilt 1870).
1802 – Saint Wendreda's church bells recast at Downham Market.
1808 – Baptist Sunday School established.
1821 – Particular Baptist Church built (another built in 1849).
1821 – Strict Baptist Church built (rebuilt 1835).
1827 – National Schools and Guildhall erected in High Street.
1829 – Wesleyan Methodists opened a chapel in High Street (rebuilt 1829).
1832 – March became a post town.
1836 – Exotic gardens opened in High Street.
1836 – Independent Congregational Church opened.
1846(?) – Unregistered gas works built.
1846 – The railway came to March (Ely to Peterborough line).
1847–8 – Lines from March to Wisbech and Saint Ives opened.
1847 – Steam mill installed at Acre wharf.
1849 – March assailed by diseases of the worst kind (441 deaths).
1850 – Town bridge opened.
1856 – Doddington Rectory Division Act: separates chapelry of March from Doddington. Later, Saint Wendreda's became a parish in its own right and other parishes formed: Saint John 1872; Saint Mary 1873; Saint Peter 1881.
1867 – Rail lines from March to Spalding opened.
1870 – Telegraph service first provided.
1873–1874 – School built in Dartford Road.
1889 – School built at West Fen (Whittlesey Road).
1891 – Saint Mary Magdalen church built at West Fen.
1900–1904 – Salvation Army established at March.
1901 – Town Hall and clock tower erected.
1908 – Telephone service provided.
1908 – County Hall built.
1912 – Roman Catholic church opened in Saint John's Road.
1921–1922 – Three per cent of males at March employed at railway centre. Twenty-eight per cent employed on the land.
1927 – County Hall enlarged.
1929 – "Up" yard built at Whitemoor.
1933 – "Down" yard built at Whitemoor for £300,000. Railway complex hailed as "March's claim to world fame."
1934 – Hereward Secondary School erected. (First building in Cambridgeshire to have a flat roof).
1937 – Further extension to County Hall.

1940 – Seven high explosive bombs on railway line at Badgeney Road.

1940 – One hundred incendiary bombs fell on Norwood Chase and twelve high explosive bombs on Graysmoor.

1941 – Two high explosive bombs at Stags Holt decoy lights. Four high explosives at Glassmoor. Fifty incendiary bombs at Whittlesey Road. Five high explosive bombs at Grandford.

1941 – Enemy aircraft machine gunned railway crossing, Wisbech Road. The town of March machine gunned. Ten high explosives on railway line near March. Five high explosive and several incendiary bombs fell at Flaggrass Hill, March. Most of the bombing incidents were in the vicinity of Whitemoor marshalling yard.

1942 – Two high explosive bombs at Stow Fen and Fifties Farm, March. Railway property damaged.

1939–1945 – During this period twenty enemy and allied aircraft crashed within a 15 mile radius of March.

1942 – Norwood Road bombed. Several killed and injured.

1942 – Wellington bomber crashed near Whitemoor "hump," setting coal trucks alight. Crew killed.

1942 – March and district raised £220,000 for the hull of P52 submarine.

1943 – £200,000 raised, sufficient for sixteen Spitfire fighters and three Lancaster bombers.

1943 – War Weapons Week. March raised £117,102.

1944 – £202,000 raised at March during "Salute The Soldier Week."

1944 – Armada of gliders filled the sky above March en route for Arnhem. One crashed near the town.

1944 – Short Stirling bomber crashed south west of Saint Wendreda's church. Pilot killed and Royal Observer Corps post saturated with burning fuel.

1944 – Flying bomb exploded in field near Town End.

POST—WAR YEARS

Roman coins and skeletons discovered at March ☆ Marshalling yards run down ☆ Industrial sites at Hostmoor, Longhill and Century Way established ☆ Swimming pool and riverside park developed ☆ Neale - Wade Comprehensive and Cavalry Barn schools erected ☆ Closure of High School, Grammar School, Hereward School and Dartford Road School.

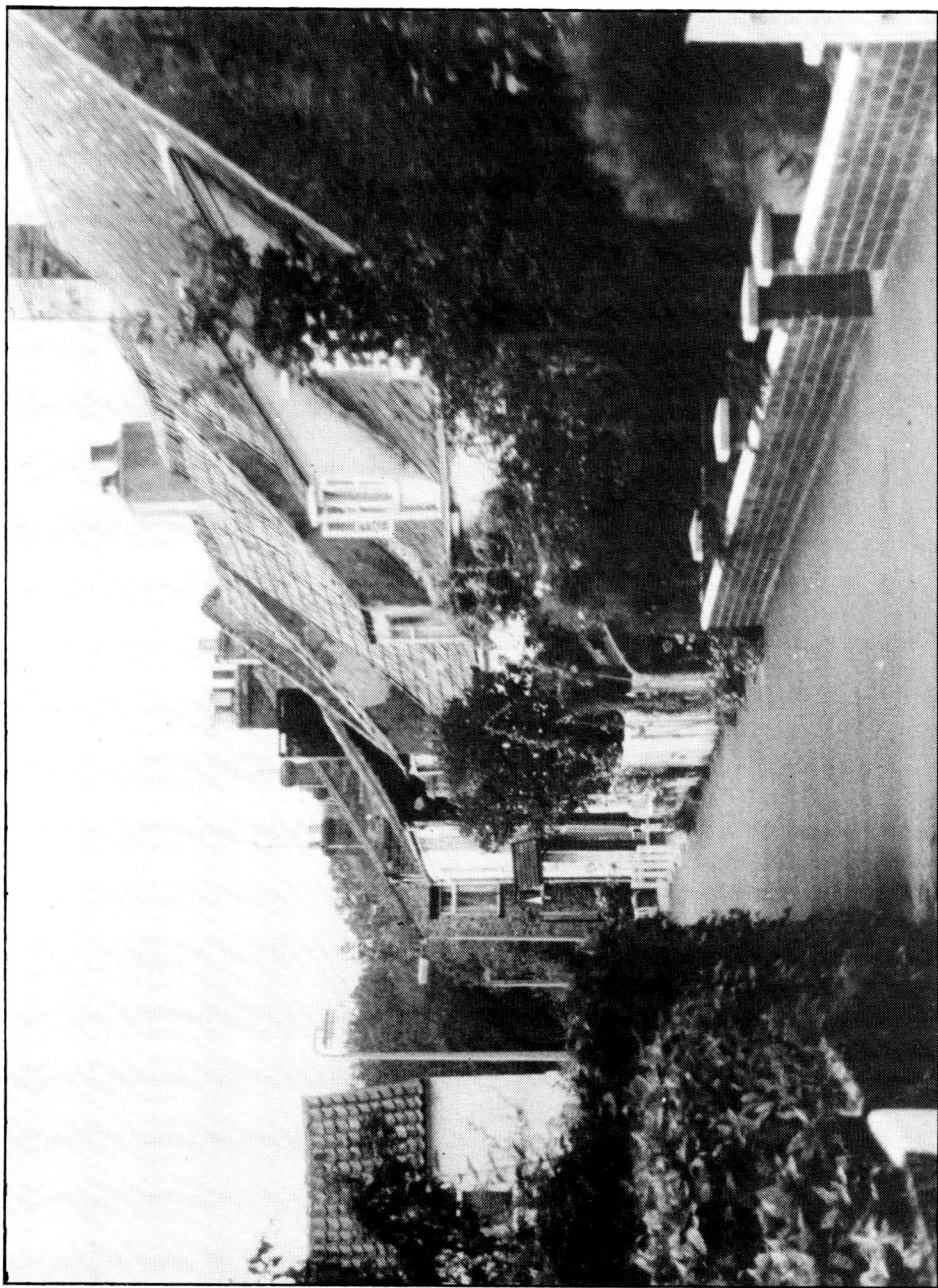

Picturesque West End, March, an ancient residential area.

MEMORIES OF WHITEMOOR

"AT FIRST I did not imagine that March had little to distinguish it from a hundred other small country towns. I was wrong. I had not been there long before I became aware that mixed among the ordinary people in the street was a surprising number of men in blue overalls, wearing black peaked caps and carrying dinner-pails. They were, I discovered, railwaymen. March was, I was told with a great deal of pride, an important railway junction, and possibly the largest marshalling yard in Europe . . .

"Before me were what seemed to be miles and miles of railway lines, as though all the sidings in the country had gathered together for conference . . . Strings of trucks clanging behind panting engines. I climbed into the (control) tower. The room at the top was walled with glass so that a view of the whole yards swept before me as I turned round. It reminded me of a ship's bridge and the inside of a signal box. The technical account which was given to me of the mechanism of the marshalling yards was remarkable for the recurrence of the words "automatic" and "Westinghouse brakes."

"Have you ever wondered how a truck of coal from Durham finally reaches a coal merchant in Dorchester? It is March which is mainly responsible for the truck getting to Dorchester. It reaches March and there the truck with hundreds of others are shunted up onto a high embankment in "runs" of about fifty trucks . . . The truck from Durham for Dorchester runs down, bumps across the points which are controlled by men in the tower, and glides into the bay for Dorchester trucks.

"And so the shunting goes on all day and all night at March, hundreds of trucks passing down the incline and into their respective bays . . . Sometimes they are for districts, like the west of England, or London; but all goods traffic coming from the north for the south passes through a sifting process at March.

"It is a keen railway brain that controls goods traffic. Loudspeakers boom instructions to the brakemen (and sometimes send out unofficial information about the winner of the four-thirty). Signals clank up and down, and the passing furnace of an engine shows driver and stoker like a couple of unfortunates in a living hell of their own. Wherever you go in March you cannot escape the sound of hissing steam from locomotives and the distant clank of trucks.

"I stood beside the controller in the tower. Before him was a little map of the yard with red and green lights that twinkled as the running trucks passed over the points . . .

"Ready to take the strawberry run, Dick?"

"O.K." shouted the controller into his mouthpiece and, as he turned round he saw the mystified look on my face. It was still winter almost and strawberries were a long way off.

"Strawberries?" I asked.

He laughed. "Not real ones. You see we have nicknames for the regular loads that come in, and we always get a trainfull of trucks about five each evening from the brickworks up Peterborough way. We call the bricks strawberries."

"As I left the tower the trucks of bricks were thundering down the incline, automatically being braked as they passed over the points, and then sliding away into the dusk where the waiting truckmen jump upon them as they pass and, sitting precariously on the long brake handles, ride with them for a while braking the speed to prevent one truck from bumping too violently into its fellows in the bay."

Such was the hey-day of March.

Victor Canning.
Reprinted from Everyman's England (1936).

L.N.E.R. 2-8-0- No. 2430 pictured at March Shed, 1934.
Colin Bedford's collection of railway photographs)